LIFE WITHOUT...

by
Ralph Hunter

James Kay Publishing

Tulsa, Oklahoma

Life Without…
ISBN 978-1-943245-12-3

www.jameskaypublishing.com

e-mail: sales@jameskaypublishing.com

Scriptures are quoted from the King James Version
unless otherwise indicated.

Cover design by JKP
Photos Provided by Ralph Hunter

Dedication

To the men that have served, and now serve, as the bishops of the congregation of the Lord's church that meets in Owasso since 1984, is this book dedicated to them for providing the means and encouragement to take the wonderful news of Jesus, to a multitude of lost souls in the jails and prisons, not only in the state of Oklahoma, but to other states (literally from coast-to-coast) in the U.S.A. For more than 30 years they have sent, and continue to send, the gospel to the lost. (To fulfill Christ's desire stated in Luke 19:10.)

Ralph Hunter

Disclaimer

I have endeavored to recreate events, locations, & conversations from my present recollection of them. Names and locations have been changed so as to not identify any particular inmate, group of inmates, or their family members. Context of situations have been altered to help keep this so. As this book has been in the planning stages for many years, verbal permission to include portions of letters and correspondence were received at the time. The publisher and the author herby state that any resemblance to any event relating to any one actual person or group of persons, living or dead, is entirely coincidental.

Ralph Hunter

Table of Contents

LIFE WITHOUT...

Introduction

In 1955, Wyatt Sawyer wrote a book titled, "Must the Young Die Too?" That publication chronicled the life of one individual and the consequence of his actions. This book will not deal with just one person, but with many. Every story (chapter) will in fact be taken from the life of an individual (or individuals) with whom I have had personal contact, yet many different men and women have repeated the same theme to me as I have spent over 28 years going into jails and prisons to teach the Gospel of Christ to the incarcerated. It is an absolute that Christ came into the world to seek and save sinners (Luke 19:10), and it is just as certain that those confined to prison cells fit both conditions; (1) sinners (2) whom the Lord desires to be saved. (II Peter 3:9)

The title of this writing comes from the phrase that is heard or read almost every day on news broadcasts and in newspapers. A jury will be reported as handing down a sentence of, "Life without the possibility of parole". But there are literally thousands who go through life without certain things, some of these we will see are things involving those that are incarcerated and some will be the things that preceded their confinement. We will attempt to address at least some of these through the lives of souls that it has been my lot to meet in the last two decades. You will read of real people, with real problems yet without knowing just one person, for the same thing lacking in each of these lives written about could be photocopied in the lives of hundreds of others. Many of the inmates that I talked with and told them about my intention to write this book asked, "Where will I be in the book?" or "Will I be in the book?" The answer of course is that they may only see themselves in the context of what their life is (or was) without.

There are of course things that inmates will tell us about, their lives as they live in the various correctional facilities, that to the everyday citizen (the inmates would speak of, "those in the free world") might not even think about. The first several chapters of this book will deal with "life without" the things that led up to incarceration, and the last few chapters will deal with things which on the outside are common, taken for granted, joys, privileges, desires and yes even what we consider necessities.

Ralph Hunter

PREFACE:

It would be very difficult to find anyone of us who has not at some time talked to, or known, a convicted felon. We may have not known it, we might not have any idea of how many we have met, but it would be rare indeed for anyone of us to not have had some kind of contact with such a person. We just don't have a "life without" having some experience of meeting an ex-convict. It might well be that we have never been to a jail or prison where all 'the bad guys are' but there are many who have served their sentences and are in our society daily.

As one who chose to spend my life preaching the Gospel, I had no idea where that might lead. It was not long after Shirley and I married, as we started working with a small congregation in Kansas, that I had my first experience with 'going to jail'. A couple who came to attend worship with us (not members of the church) became involved with writing bad checks and asked that I would go with them as they had to face their judgment. At the next place we served the church, I came in contact with a relative of a teenager who was in the county jail and asked me to go and visit him. Not many years passed before I was asked by a mother at another congregation where I was preaching to go and talk with her son that was in jail.

It was while I was with this same congregation that I served a year as president in the Kiwanis Club. That year a project of the club involved bringing an ex-offender to speak to the high school students concerning the hideousness of drug use. In that ex-offenders presentation he made the statement, "I would far rather be given a death sentence than to have a sentence of life without parole."

In all these events, I still had a "life without" any thought of spending between a fourth and a third of the years of my life going into jails and prisons on a full-time basis to teach Bible there. But indeed, that has been a rewarding part of my life.

While preaching in Collinsville, Oklahoma, a member there was a jailer in the Tulsa County Jail. He asked if I would be afraid to go and talk to a young man that was awaiting trial for murder but wanted to talk to someone about his soul. For over a year I went into that facility every Tuesday to study God's Word with him. It was not long before he asked if I would talk with another inmate who was interested in the Bible study he was doing. After almost a year studying with these two men, they were both convicted and sent to the same correctional center near Stringtown, Oklahoma. As we corresponded and Bible lessons were sent to these two, it was not unusual for one or the other to make a request for the lessons to be sent to some other inmate on that yard. I soon had 19 students taking the courses and then the request came, "Why can't you come here and have a class like we had in the county jail?" My answer was that I would start making the arrangements to do just that. In the fall of 1986 the chaplain allowed time for us to have our first class. In that first Tuesday night class we had 18 souls in attendance, and for the next 16 years I had no thoughts of having a "life without" teaching the Word of God in correctional facilities.

All of the stories in these pages are from letters or personal conversations from or with real men and women it has been my lot to have personally had opportunity to talk or correspond with, about the God of heaven and His Son. All the characters written about are very real people, but not their real names. There are lengthy quotations from some, and from some just a few lines. But I hope to bring all their thoughts to life that we might all see and learn from the tragic mistakes that mankind has made throughout all history.

Through the years opportunity was granted to me to teach in some nine different state facilities, six county jails, and one federal facility, as well as being in contact by mail with inmates from at least a dozen more places across the nation. It is remarkable that I have heard the same stories, the same backgrounds, the same kinds of ungodliness, and the same results from hundreds of different souls in all these facilities. All of the stories in these pages are from letters or personal conversations from or with real men and women it has been my lot to have personally had opportunity to talk or correspond with, about the God of heaven and His Son. All the characters written about are very real people, but not their real names. There are lengthy quotations from some, and from some just a few lines. But I hope to bring all their thoughts to life that we might all see and learn from the tragic mistakes that mankind has made throughout all history.

In addition to meeting literally hundreds if not thousands of men and women that have become known because of their crimes, I have been educated in the language of the inmates and have learned a great deal about the correctional system that was foreign to me before this work was granted to me to perform. Perhaps many that might read this book already are familiar with the different security levels, but many are not. Before I started in jail/ prison evangelism my idea of prison in Oklahoma was like so many, "The prison was at McAlester." In reality there are over 70 different facilities in our state. Some are classified as 'Maximum' such as Oklahoma State Penitentiary in McAlester or Oklahoma State Reformatory in Granit. Some are 'Medium' as is the one at Lexington where there is freedom to move about on the prison yard while still within the fences of the facility. Others are 'Minimum' security level where there may not be any fences at all and inmates are often taken out to such work as cleaning up trash along highways. There are also even lower level security units like work centers where the inmates are under supervision, even while they might be out working in a 'public' job.

The following list are those facilities I have had the opportunity to present the Gospel:

The old Tulsa County Jail. (To both male and female inmates.)

David L. Moss Criminal Justice Center (Tulsa County Jail.) This new county jail is divided into some twenty-two 'pods' with 96 beds in each pod. I have had the privilege of teaching (only the men's pods) in Pods 4; 5; 6; 12, as well as being allowed to visit inmates in the 'SEGREGATED' cells. These are cells where men are placed after convictions, and waiting to be transported to the state facilities.

For a short time about two (2) months I was allowed to meet in the chapel area with female inmates that were brought out of the female side of David L. Moss C.J.C. on Wednesday evenings for an hour. (Sometimes there were as many as 40 to 50 in these classes.)

Jess Dunn Correctional Center (Taft, Oklahoma) A minimum-security facility; when we first started, this was a 'co-ed' facility.

John Lillie C.C. (Boley, Oklahoma), for services and Bible study from 5 till 7 p.m. every Sunday.

Lexington (L.A.R.C.), Lexington, Okla. For two-hour Bible study on Mondays 10 a.m. – 12 noon.

Joseph Harp C.C (about three miles from L.A.R.C) for Bible study 2 – 4 p.m. Mondays.

Back to Lexington (Rex Thompson C.C. a minimum unit outside the fence) 7- 9 p.m.

Mack Alford (Stringtown, Oklahoma), medium unit, 9 a.m. – 5 p.m. every Monday.

Mack Alford minimum 6 – 8 p.m. Mondays.

M.A.C.C. minimum yard 9 a.m. 5 p.m. Tuesdays.

M.A.C.C. medium yard 6 – 8 p.m. every Tuesday.

Ouachita Correctional Center (less than a dozen visits).

Tulsa Adult Detention Center Thursdays afternoons.

Turley C.C. (female) and Avelone Center (male)
work centers.

Oklahoma, Kingfisher, Haskell, McCurtain,
Muskogee, Creek, Washington, and
Sequoyah county jails.

Who are some of these people that I have met in the correctional facilities over the years? Some of course I have never met in person, only by correspondence, but none the less still on a very personal basis. There are those that became well known throughout the nation because of the crimes committed, while others are famous just here in Oklahoma. Others might only be known by a few 'home town' citizens.

Among those that the whole country knows about would be a 'serial killer' that many comments have been made by multitudes of people, not only in our nation, but also throughout the world. This man's name has been spoken by many in anger, disgust, ridicule, and unbelief that someone could commit such a crime and as the target of vile jokes. Politicians, television comedians, televangelist, as well as news commentators have brought up his name and crime for years even after his death.

There would be Oklahomans that caused the state to be held in shock and fear as the news of their crimes were publicized in statewide radio and TV stations. Among those will be people like the man who escaped from the Oklahoma State Penitentiary twice, this same individual having spent many years on 'Death Row' before having his sentence commuted to a life sentence. All of these events placed on the pages of the two largest newspapers in the state of Oklahoma.

Then some of the stories will be of people that most of the state of Oklahoma's population have not read or heard about. The locals from the hometowns of these inmates might have known about (if the town was small enough) their crimes, but outside of their local communities nothing was ever mentioned in the media. This group is only known as a part of a very large prison population that tax dollars have to be spent to keep incarcerated.

Chapter 1

Life Without …
Remembering Hearing a Baby Cry!

In my first year or so of work in jail/prison evangelism as a volunteer in the Correctional System, a young man serving a life sentence sent me this short essay.

"PRISON IS A PLACE"

1. *Prison is a place where the first prisoner you see looks like an All-American college boy, and you are surprised. Later you're disgusted, because people on the outside still have the same prejudices about prisoners that you used to have.*

2. *Prison is a place where you write letters and can't think of anything to say. Where you gradually write fewer and fewer letters and finally stop writing altogether.*

3. *Prison is a place where hopes spring eternal. Where each parole appearance means a chance to get out even if the odds are hopelessly against you.*

4. *Prison is a place where you learn that nobody needs you; that the outside world goes on without you.*

5. *Prison is a place where you can go for years without feeling the touch of a human hand. Where you can go for months without hearing a kind word. It's a place where your friendships are shallow and you know it.*

6. *Prison is a place where you feel sorry for yourself, then you get disgusted with yourself for feeling sorry for yourself, then you get mad for feeling disgusted, then you try to mentally change the subject.*

7. *Prison is a place where you forget the sound of a BABY CRYING (emphasis mine. rdh) You forget the sound of a dog's bark, even the sound of the dial tone of a telephone.*

8. *Prison is a place where you see men that you do not admire and wonder if you are like them. It's a place where you strive to remain civilized, but where you lose ground and know it.*

9. *Prison is a place where if you are married you watch your marriage die. It is a place where you learn that you stop blaming your wife for wanting a real man instead of a fading memory of one.*

10. *Prison is a place where you go to bed before you're tired. Where you pull the blanket over your head when you're not even cold. It's a place where you escape by reading, by playing cards, by dreaming, or by going mad."*

Many of these thoughts "Wayne" wrote to me were brought back again and again in my mind as I would spend hours with inmates on the prison yards, and I will borrow some of them as topics we will discuss.

The first one with which I will deal, the thought that he wrote about forgetting, "The sound of a baby crying." This is of course not a physical truism, but rather an emotional one for there are many times when wives have brought their

"My youngest will be a young man before I can go back to my home and will he even know me as his father? I will not get to hold him when he falls and has a little hurt that needs a good application of TLC that a daddy should give."

small children to 'see Daddy' and the sound of a crying child echoes across the facility yard. The scene (I saw it played out many times) of a family leaving after a visit and a child sobbing with words such as, "Daddy I love you, why can't you come home with us?" is a very emotional one. I remember a family leaving and I heard the little boy, I would guess about 4 or 5, say to his daddy, "You could climb over the fence and meet us at the car." (Keep in mind the fence is some 12 feet high with another 4 feet of razor wire rolls on top.)

An inmate, from another state serving a relative short sentence (20 years), asked if I could come to his cell and talk with him about things concerning his family. He had three children, the youngest not yet two. With tears running down his cheeks, he spoke of the feeling that he might never see his children again. His family lived almost a thousand miles away and of course without 'a bread winner' in the home would not be able financially to make the trip to see him. He said as we talked, "My youngest will be a young man before I can go back to my home and will he even know me as his father? I will not get to hold him when he falls and has a little hurt that needs a good application of TLC that a daddy should give." As our conversation continued, as well as his tears, he kept repeating, "Oh, how foolish, how foolish! Why did I think that the money I would make by transporting those drugs would make me happy?"

When this young man said this, it brought to mind the words written in the Colossian book of the New Testament (Chapter 3 verse 1), *"If you then be risen with Christ, seek those things which are above, where Christ sits on the right hand of God."* And also the words spoken by Jesus about if a man should gain the whole world yet loose his soul, it would not be profitable to him. Not only had this young man lost his freedom but also now his concern was that he was losing his family.

This is not an unusual thing to happen when one is incarcerated, in reality there are perhaps more marriages that break up than stay together among those that are imprisoned. I do not have exact statistics about this, but the number of times I have been approached by inmates asking if I could talk with wives or husbands to try to keep those mates on the outside from filing for divorce are legion.

It was not only men that came talking about losing their

families, but women as well. I visited a young lady about 25 to 30 years of age, in the county jail for approximately 30 months, the mother of three children ranging in age 2 to 8. "Judy" had been living with a man not her husband that was charged with killing their infant son. The charge against Judy was, "failure to protect a minor" and her prison sentence was dependent on the outcome of the man's trial. It was for this reason that there was such a long stay in the county jail.

While in the county jail, Judy's parents were given guardianship of the children. The grandparents lived some 100 miles or so from Tulsa and tried to bring the children to see her about once a month. The rules of the correctional facility would allow only one grandparent and one child per visit. You can understand then the hardship on Judy's parents.

It was always very noticeable to me when I would make my weekly visit with her that she had had a visit from one of her children. She did not have to tell me that such an event had occurred for she would greet me with a big smile on her face, but then when she would tell me which child had been to visit, the tears would appear. There would be several minutes of having to tell me how much she missed her family. It would be perhaps as much as 10 minutes before we could get into our Bible study.

Finally, when she was sentenced and was handed over to the Department of Corrections, she was placed in the Mabel Basset Center in Oklahoma City. However, it was not long after that, Oklahoma Corrections sent many inmates to private prisons in Texas and Judy was placed in a private prison in San Antonio. One of her letters to me had this message:

> "I thought it was hard to be without my kids when I had to go a month or so without seeing any of them, but it is terrible not being able to see them for almost a year now. I wonder if they will even remember me when I get out?"

Another inmate wrote the following:

> "I'm trying to adapt to this life but it is not easy; I do pray about it every day and I study from the word. However, I still feel so alone at times. I feel like no one cares, but I know that they do. I know that there are people praying for me and that means a lot. I know that my parents are behind me, but what hurts is that I have lost my family. I know it is my fault, but it still hurts. How nice it would be if I could just turn back the clock a couple of years and turn down that lure of money that was offered me to transport those drugs."

As I read this letter from "Ramon Sanchez" I could not help but think of the passage of scripture in I Timothy 6:10, *"For the love of money is the root of all evil: which while some covet after, they have erred from the faith, and pierced themselves through with many sorrows."* Ramon often talked with me about his children. He had four, twins, that seemed to be his pride and joy. On one occasion his words to me were, "Just to think that I sold them (drugs) for money so I could come to Durant to play Bingo to make more money."[1] For the love of money, he had lost being with these beloved twins for a dozen years. As he spoke I could not help but think of Paul's words as recorded in Ephesians 5:5, *"..., that no fornicator, nor unclean person, nor* <u>*covetous man, who is an idolater*</u>*, hath any inheritance in the kingdom of Christ, and of God."*

---

[1] He was speaking about what he had lost by transporting drugs across the state borders of _____ & _____ for money.

Chapter 2

Life Without…
A Knowledge of God's Word

The prophet of old speaking the words of Jehovah by inspiration wrote, *"My people are destroyed for lack of knowledge:"* (Hosea 4:6a) as a message to Israel. Isaiah wrote saying, *"Therefore my people are gone into captivity, because they have no knowledge; and there honourable men are famished, and their multitude dried up with thirst."* (Isaiah 5:13) Jesus is quoted by John the apostle in his gospel saying, *"No man can come to me, except the Father which hath sent me draw him: and I will raise him up in the last day. It is written in the prophets, And they shall all be taught of God. Every man therefore that hath heard, and hath learned of the Father, cometh unto me."* (6:44 – 45)

The correctional officer called out, "Bible study" in the tank of the county jail, and after some ten minutes no one had come to the area where the class was to be held. As I waited the officer said, "Doesn't look like you have anyone interested!" I responded with a comment something like, "This is a trustee unit is it not? And maybe it is not time for some to be back in from work. I will just wait a little longer to see if someone might come in and want to study." It was just a few minutes and the big steel sliding door opened and a middle-aged fellow walked in. He looked over into the small room where the class was held each week and asked, "What is this?" My reply was that it was just a Bible study. He wanted to know if he could be a part of it. In a heartbeat, my answer shot back, "Absolutely!"

"Curtis" informed me that he had worked in the porno film industry out in California, and said that he had seen Bibles before, but had never opened one to see what was in it. Having been arrested and placed in the county jail with nothing to do all day so he picked up a ragged Bible. One that had been more than just used, rather it had been abused by being thrown around more than once or twice. Curtis went to his cell and returned with the book, saying that he had tried to read it, but could not understand a thing it was saying. With just the two of us in the meeting we opened the old tattered book to the first chapter of Genesis and started looking at the creation story. The questions came rapidly from Curtis' lips as we turned from the first epistle of Moses, *"In the beginning God created the heaven and the earth."* (1:1), to the Psalmists declaration in chapter 33, *"By the word of the Lord were the heavens made; and all the host of them by the breath of His mouth. He gathered the waters of the sea together as an heap: He layeth up the depth in storehouses. Let all the earth fear the Lord: let all the inhabitants of the world stand in awe of Him. For He spake, and it was done; He commanded, and it stood fast."* (verses 6 – 9), to John's gospel chapter 1, *"In the begging was the Word, and the Word was with God, and the Word was God. The same was in the beginning with God. All things were made by Him; and without Him was not any thing made that was made."* (verses 1 – 3) and then to Hebrews 1:1 – 2 *"God, who at sundry times and in divers manners spake in times past unto the fathers by the prophets, hath in this last days spoken unto us by his Son, whom he hath appointed heir of all things, by whom also he made the worlds;"* connecting all the passages dealing with the creation of our world, and who was involved. "Is there always such a correlation of all the things in the Bible?" he asked. My response was in the affirmative, and I spent the next hour telling the wonderful story of Deity's desire for His creation to be saved (I Peter 3:9) even after man has sinned (Romans 3:23) and how that was revealed in this book that is called the Bible.

The thought came to me as Curtis posed this inquiry, that this was much like Philip asking the Ethiopian if he understood what he was reading (Acts 8 and verse 30) The difference was of course that the Ethiopian was a religious man returning from a religious gathering in Jerusalem, reading the scriptures. Curtis had never read the Holy writings. It was a joy to see the look of amazement on Curtis' face as we examined the writings of inspired men, and they came into focus in his mind. It was much like the day my oldest son came home from school in the first grade and on that day the key to understanding how letters began to make sense to him as words. That day will always be etched in my memory as I picked Stephen up from school, and his eyes were twinkling with excitement as he said, "Let me read this story to you." He could hardly wait to get home so he could show his mother that he could read. This was the same type of excitement that I saw in Curtis' eyes and heard in his voice as the scriptures were made real to him for the first time in his life.

As it drew close to the time for 'Lock Down' Curtis was not out of questions. The question that he asked as the officer stood at the door waiting for him to go to his cell was, "When will you be back and can we study some more?" Curtis left the room expressing this thought: "I had no idea that the Bible made so much sense!"

It was not just the men that were confined in the steel doors of correctional facilities, but the female inmates were restricted in the cells as well as their knowledge of God's Word. Like Curtis, a lady we will know as "Lidia" sent me a note after I left a 15 lesson Bible course with her. I had less than an hour to talk with the group of about 25 in that first meeting. The following is her first note that she enclosed with the lessons.

> "Here are the 1st five Bible studies. I enjoyed them immensely and looking forward to the next ones. I must tell you, I am 40 years old and never knew learning about the Lord could be so enjoyable. I want to learn more and more every day. Thank you for your help. GOD BLESS."

The week after the class period in which I met Lidia, she was sentenced and sent to Ouachita Correctional Center at Hodgen, Oklahoma. I received 3 more notes from her, the third (in part) contained this message:

> "Are you acquainted with a man named Phil Powers? (I know Phil,

> and have worked with him through
> the years in connection with jail/
> prison efforts. *rdh*) He is the pastor of
> Poteau Church of Christ. ...... Well
> as you see, I am ready for some more
> studies. I enjoy them very much. I'll
> be waiting patiently for them. ......
> In the King's name, Lidia"

It was a real joy to me knowing Lidia had been placed where she could continue to study under a faithful teacher of the Lord's way. It has been more than 20 years since I last heard from, or about her.

In the third year of our working in the correctional facilities, a young man came into our class with a hand-tooled leather Bible cover that he had made in the leather shop and handed it to me. I looked it over and handed it back toward him, but he said that it was for me. I have carried my Bible with that cover many miles, having received many comments and questions about it. But one comment stands out in my mind, a comment made by a rather aged man. He asked if he could look at my Bible and the cover, and for what seemed like a minute or two, his face having a look on it as if in deep thought. After a long period of silence, he said, "I wish I had dedicated myself to have wrapped the Word of God in my life like this cover has." As we continued our conversation "Bob" went on to say that he could tell by the well-worn leather that it had not been setting on a shelf and he added, "And from the look of the pages of the book inside that cover those pages have been turned many times."

I took that as a great compliment and told him so then asked him, "Bob, do you not think that you could start now and dedicate yourself to learning what the Bible has revealed for you? If you have the desire, you certainly have time available to you to study these truths for yourself. For as long as you live you have the opportunity to learn God's Word that He has provided for you." A grin crossed his face as he said something like, "Do you really think I could learn something as old as I am?" For perhaps two years Bob was in our class every week as well as visiting with me many hours in his cell during 'lock down' time. The young man who gave a gift in one correctional facility had no idea that that piece of leather would provide such an opportunity to present the words that it would wrap around an old man's life hopefully for eternity. Bob was transferred from that facility after those two years and I

There are many who come into the prison system, just like there are many in the free world, who think they know the Bible, or talk about knowing what the Word of God says. But the truth is that they know very little of what the Word really says.

lost contact with him, but is my prayer that he continued to wrap himself in the Word of the Lord.

There are many who come into the prison system, just like there are many in the free world, who think they know the Bible, or talk about knowing what the Word of God says. But the truth is that they know very little of what the Word really says.

If it were not so eternally tragic it would almost be humorous to listen to some of the ideas presented. Most of the teaching that came from these fellows is 'wishful thinking' on their part, perhaps to give them a ray of hope. Looking back at a statement that Wayne made, remember the list he made as I recorded in chapter 1, "Prison Is a Place". The third point he made was: "Prison was a place where hopes spring eternal. Where each parole appearance means a chance to get out even if the odds are hopelessly against you." Because of this kind of thinking I had the following experiences.

One individual that I will always remember was a middle-aged man that had many of his fellow inmates believing that the Lord had told him that he would be home before the end of the year. I first met "Sam" in April or May and it did not take us long to get on the subject of 'special revelation'. It was less than an hour after meeting him that he told me how the Lord had spoken to him with the message that he would be home for Christmas of that year.

It is important just here to point out that this was in 1987 and Sam had three (3) one hundred year sentences (in the language of inmates, 'running wild') to be served consecutively, plus two 20 year sentences. Also, Sam had served less than 5 years of these sentences. As I write this, Sam is still incarcerated and has never been brought up for parole consideration in the 15 years since.

When Sam and I began our discussion, he became argumentative after just a short time. The longer we talked, the louder he became. The veins in his neck were very visible and his face grew redder by the moment. For fear that the officers would think that some sort of argument or fight was about to break out I told him that we would get together some other time to continue the subject. And indeed we did, many times over the next ten or twelve months.

The very sad result of such teaching is that when there are people as charismatic (or threatening) as this man was, many will follow without searching the Word of God for the truth that is revealed. I would often ask those that would follow men of such persuasion to study Deuteronomy 18:28 with me. *"When a prophet speaks in the name of the Lord, if the thing follows not, nor come to pass, that is the thing which the Lord hath not spoken, but the prophet hath spoken it presumptuously; thou shall not be afraid of him."*

> Often times I would present the thought to such individuals that the guilt of sins can be forgiven, but the consequences of such actions cannot be reversed.

Sam's concept was not one of his own. Many times I would have inmates come to me with the same kind of thoughts. Though there were many different wordings, yet the same general idea was, "The Lord is going to get me out soon." To the men that approached me with this I would ask them, "Did the Lord put you in here?" Often times I would present the thought to such individuals that the guilt of sins can be forgiven, but the consequences of such actions cannot be reversed. Of course, there sometimes is offered 'grace' by the offended (the state as in the case of inmates) but that is wholly left up to the law of the land. At any rate, the offense is never undone. I would often use the example of King David in teaching inmates that followed after such teachings. Of course, we remember that David committed the sins of adultery, murder (causing the husband to be killed), disobeying the Lord by recounting the people, as well as misusing the Lord's tabernacle.

We know that David was spoken of as a man after God's heart, and this of course would have to have meant that he had forgiveness of the Father, but the results of his sins were always present. Thus, I taught that just because one might obey the Lord and be forgiven in the sight of the Divine it did not follow that they (the inmate) would be free from having to pay for the offenses they had committed against humanity. One inmate learned this lesson well. The following statements come from his pen:

> "The (inmate's name) you've read about on these pages, cold, violent, a murderer many times over, is dead and gone, to never live again. ...... Society can hold my body in prison until it rots and turns to dust. I do not care, for to my Heavenly Father, a lost son has come home."

As with the case of Sam's teaching, the same kind of following would come about when someone thought that if they could just use the Bible, there might be some way around a rule one might not like. This came to my attention in a very real and amusing way, yet as a shock.

In the late '80s and early '90s one of the 'opps' of the Department of Correction was that an inmate must be clean-shaven and no long hair. This rule could be waived if there were religious convictions, such as the Native American (Indian), that was a codified teaching of a recognized religious group. In about 1995 this rule was changed and no longer were there these restrictions.

Why bring this to your attention when talking about inmates misunderstanding or misusing scriptures? To borrow a phrase, "A funny thing happened to me on the way to work..." As I came through the control center to check in for the day, the Captain on duty handed me a letter. (It was a strange feeling to get mail at the prison. Maybe I had been coming for too long a time.) I noticed a smile as the officer handed me the letter and I asked him, "What's this?" When I read it, it was a notice that I had been named in a lawsuit by an inmate.

When the chaplain was gone, either by having appointments at other facilities or on vacation, I often was called on to sit in when a request for a waiver from an inmate was made to the staff. These meetings were before three staff members: The deputy warden, the unit manager of the inmate's unit and the chaplain. All three had responsibility to question the one making such a request and then to approve or deny that request, based on the compliance of the written guidelines. As a general rule, if any one of the three staff members denied the request, such request was sent to the warden for a final decision and was thus denied. The chaplain's role of course was to note the rules of the religious group that the one making the request said he was following.

The inmate (I did not know this person, and don't remember his name) that had filed a lawsuit against me, had made a request for such a waver to not have to cut his hair. His argument for such a waver was this: "The Bible says not to cut the hair or beard," and he had written as a reference on the request two passages. Leviticus 19:27, *"You shall not round the corners of your heads, neither shalt thou mar the corners of thy beard."* and Leviticus 21:5, *"They shall not make baldness upon their head, neither shall thy shave off the corner of their beard."* Someone on the yard had come upon these two passages and thought they would be a 'surefire, foolproof' means of getting around the rule of short hair and no facial hair.

After the two staff members and I listened on this occasion, the deputy warden turned to me and asked if I had any questions to address to the inmate. The following was my response. "You have brought to our attention the passages from Leviticus chapters 19 and 21 as your justification on a religious basis for not cutting your hair. However, you did not complete the passage in 21:5 and you stopped short of reading the continued thoughts of 19:27 in the following verse. At which time I picked up my Bible (which I had brought into the meeting to be sure to make my point clear) and read the two passages I had brought to the inmate's attention. In 19:28, *"Ye shall not make any cuttings in your flesh for the dead, nor print any marks upon you:"* and in 21:5 the completion of that verse is, *"nor make any cuttings in their flesh."* When I had finished reading these passages I said something like, "Your arms are covered with tattoos, does that not count in your 'religious' convictions?" The inmate made no comment.

I could not help but notice the expressions on the faces of the two staff members in the meeting. The deputy warden then explained to the prisoner that he would hear from the warden the next day as to either his request being approved or denied, and with that dismissed him from the meeting. After he left and the three of us had marked the request, approved or denied, the deputy turned to me and said that he really appreciated what I had done and that it would always be an answer for those that tried to use the Bible in a false way as a tool to escape following the rules.

It was just a few weeks later that I was informed at the front gate that I was named as a defendant in the lawsuit, having violated the man's civil rights. I went to deputy with the letter to ask what I should do about it he smiled and reached for it with the reassuring words, "Don't worry about it." I never heard anything again about the action, or do I remember ever seeing that inmate again.

Two scriptures come to mind as I think of Sam and the man that brought the lawsuit against me. The first, *"Give diligence to present thyself approved unto God, a workman that needeth not to be ashamed, handling aright the word of truth."* (I Timothy 2:15) The second, *"You do err, not knowing the scriptures, nor the power of God."* (Matthew 22:29) So many times inmates such as these two did not know the scriptures or did not handle them in a right way.

> I found many, both men and women, who did not know the scriptures, that were eager to learn and accurately use God's message in their lives.

But thanks be to God I often found the opposite to be true. I found many, both men and women, who did not know the scriptures, that were eager to learn and accurately use God's message in their lives.

Two such souls were "K.C." and a big Indian gentleman I met in one of the minimum-security facilities. K.C. had been in our Bible study and Sunday worship period for a couple of months when he brought "William", his cell mate, with him one week. William told me several months after K.C. had left that K.C. had often invited him to come and study the Bible with us but he was skeptical. When I asked the reason for his skepticism his answer was, "I was concerned about just taking the Bible only to study and K.C. said that was all you did." He told me that K.C. just kept after him to come and investigate for himself that he finally gave in and came with him. It was not long after that William obeyed the gospel and he told me later that he and K.C. spent many hours going over the lessons we studied on those Sunday afternoons. I do not know what happed to K.C. after he went back to his home in another state, but for William I followed him for three or four years after his release from prison and know that he graduated from the University of Central Oklahoma with a degree in counseling. He spoke on two or three workshops that were conducted concerning jail/prison mission work and also taught a class in the congregation in Oklahoma City where he placed membership.

BRUCE WILLIAMS
Daily Oklahoman Wed., July 14, 1993

Roger Bruce Williams, 63, of Oklahoma City, died Monday, July 12, 1993 after a long illness with cancer. Bruce was born in Perry County, Ga. to Robert & Mary Williams.

Bruce was the minister for the church of Christ and has been active in the church of Christ prison mission work since 1980. "His life was an example of how the Blood of Jesus really changes a man's heart." He is survived by hundreds of lives that he has touched. In lieu of flowers, donations are requested to be sent to the _____ church of Christ prison mission fund.

Services will be 2:30 p.m. Thursday, July 15 at _____ church of Christ with interment at Memorial Park cemetery.

The following article was written about Bruce by a gospel preacher attending the funeral.

The Tale of Two Funerals

Charles Dickens said it well when he penned, *"It was the best of times, it was the worst of times."* That pretty well describes two funerals I attended recently. One was last Thursday for Bruce Williams. The other I attended today (Monday). I did this funeral. It was for a lady I did not know. Ironically, both of the people were about same age, Bruce was 63, and the lady was 62. But these two funerals were as different as daylight and dark.

Bruce's funeral was well attended. Even though he had no living family, there must have been in excess of 400 people there. This lady had living family, but counting me, there were only 35 of us.

There was an abundance of volunteers to memorialize Bruce: two preachers, three song leaders leading nearly fifteen songs, two prayer leaders, and it looked like about twenty pall bearers. Those serving at the funeral Monday recruited and/or hired: one preacher, one singer, one organist, and no pall bearers (except the funeral home staff and three cemetery workers.)

While viewing these two funerals in my mind, I could not help thinking how wonderful Bruce's was and how sad the other was. Both of these individuals were good-hearted people. And so, I tried to find what the difference was, and the only thing I could find was a strong commitment to Christ.

In the first two-thirds of Bruce's life, he served only self. And had he died then, there would not have been even 35 people at his funeral. But he didn't die then. Rather, he was radically touched with the blood of Jesus Christ. And from that day forward, he spent his energy on serving others, sacrificing for others, and sharing the message of Christ. The man who had no family had a huge family in the people of God. The prisons of Oklahoma will never be the same because of his pioneering work in his ministry.

Though a good person, the lady who was buried had limited contact with people. She was a fine citizen. She worked hard all of her life in Civil Service. But she had only a casual acquaintance with Jesus Christ. There was no church family to surround the mourners. No one to prepare a meal for the bereaved, as you do so well. Totally alone.

The missing ingredient was Jesus Christ. The difference between a mediocre existence and a dynamic one is the Man from Galilee. A radical commitment to him and his church can mean the difference between dying alone and dying with a multitude of support and remembers.

* * *

Many years later I wrote the following article in the monthly publication about the jail/prison efforts of the Owasso church of Christ: (*rdh*)

The Deaths of Two Ex-Felons

I want to present to the readers of this newsletter, two ex-felons that are examples of why jail/prison evangelism is a worthwhile mission effort. These two ex-felons both died after completing their sentences, but both were my very close friends. Their deaths were separated by some 15 years and they were not in the same correctional facility, nor did their sentences overlap.

Bruce Williams passed away in 1993 and Ray Ingram passed away the first day of 2009. Bruce was a great influence on my getting involved in jail/prison evangelism while Ray was one that it was my joy to assist in becoming a New Testament Christian in 1988.

Ray would be likened to the man in the parable of the sower (Matthew 13:18 – 23) that received seed into the good ground and brought forth abundance in verse 23. It was shortly after I first met Ray in '88, that he began to be a constant and eager student when we met for Bible study. It was not many weeks after our first study that he requested to be baptized into Christ for the forgiveness of his sins. Much like the eunuch in the eighth chapter of Acts, Ray had many questions about this JESUS that we presented to him. He came to me and asked, "When can I be baptized?" Understanding that in prisons that it is sometimes a rather lengthy process to make arrangements to baptize an individual, I told Ray that we would get the process started as soon as possible. Making request to the Chaplain, I wondered just how long it would be, before this could be accomplished. Gratefully, when I came back to that facility the next week permission had been granted and when I told Ray, he was like the eunuch and said, "We have the water, what is stopping me from being baptized now!", and he came up from the water and from that day forward went on his way rejoicing. Of course, he did not leave the facility but everyone on the yard was fair game to him to try and teach what he had learned.

After a riot at the facility in '90, the facility was divided into two areas. One was a Medium Unit and the other classified as a Minimum Unit. Ray became the Chaplain's clerk on the Minimum side, and started conducting Bible classes in addition to the classes that we were having each Monday night. It was not long after that, that Ray had the joy of baptizing his cell-mate into Christ. And though he never again was allowed to physically do the baptizing, he did teach several others that we were able to baptize.

After his release from prison he went to the Sunset School of Preaching and has worked with the Southwest church in Ada since his graduation.

His work with that congregation has been, "JAIL/PRISON" evangelism. Ray taught in four correctional facilities a week, until his death.

I have counted it a blessing to have been a friend, as well as a brother to Ray. I will miss him immensely.

ralph

Chapter 3

Life Without...
A Proper Role Model

*"Children, obey your parents in the Lord: for this is right ......
And, you fathers, provoke not your children to wrath: but nurture
them in the chastening and
admonition of the Lord."*
writes the apostle Paul in
the sixth chapter of the
book of Ephesians. But un
-fortunately, these exhorta-
tions are not heeded on
many occasions by either
children or parents. As a
result, such cases, as the
following have been made
known to me.

"I was then sent back to prison to finish my first fifteen-year sentence before the new one would start. This time I was sent to higher security facility than I had been on the first occasion."

"As a child growing up I really
can't say that my home environment
resembled in any way what most folks
would consider a healthy and happy
one. Oh, there were some bright spots but
for the most part life within my household
was constantly taken up with enduring
pain, hardship, and basic survival. The
family consisted of my mother, two sisters
(one older and the other younger), a
drunken step-dad and myself.

As far back as I can recall I don't remember there being many times when we weren't experiencing problems in some fashion. Our step-dad was an alcoholic. There was not a single day that passed that he wasn't consuming beer. We were poor; most times we saw only two meals a day (one at home and the other the lunch served to us at school). Early on Mom would work, first at a cotton gin and then as a laundry person in a nursing home; these were minimum wage jobs, which barely got the bills paid. The old man drew a disability check but would drink it up and whatever money Mom had left after bills were paid and a small amount of food bought. Our cloths were always second hand from either the Salvation Army or Goodwill. Lots of times we didn't have socks or underwear.

Whenever the old man was good and drunk (which was almost always) he would begin to sexually molest my oldest sister and then beat on Mom for no reason than to make himself feel like a man.

School was a place that my sisters and I had frequent dreads and reservation about attending because of the cloths we wore. It was obvious to the other kids that we were poor and it seemed as though this fact made it all right in their minds to make fun of us. Sometimes I would end up in fights with kids who pushed my level of endurance to the breaking point, all because he or she (we had some female bullies) was out to muster the approval of their peers by picking on the poor kid. When all the school violence broke out in our nation I began to realize just how close I was to going over the edge during my own time in the school system.

Sometime during our early childhood, Mom started sending us to Sunday school. There was a church bus that made the rounds through the neighborhood so this made it convenient for us. I suppose that in a way Mom saw it as an opportunity to give us a small break once a week from the burden of life at home. At first I had reservations about going because I figured that I'd get the same treatment at Sunday school that I had been receiving at the public school. It turned out that was not the case at all. Instead of being teased and made fun of, my sisters and I were accepted just as any of the other kids.

It was at this time in my life that I met an older Christian gentleman by the name of Russell. He and his wife

Virginia would sometimes have us over to their home. It was Russell who taught me how to correctly write out the alphabet.

My family began to move around from house to house, this was about the time the old man's disability check was cut off. This left my Mom's minimum wage the only source of income. The drinking didn't slow down any though, and I suppose that's why we were moving around so much, because the rent and bills were not getting paid. Young minds are impressionable. I suppose that it was about this period in my life that us kids got the idea it was ok to conceal food items under our cloths when we went in the grocery store and see if we could make it outside the store with them. If we were not successful in this venture, then supper that evening was sparse. Consisting of a little fried potatoes and red beans, or one or two bologna sandwiches.

During our moving around, sometimes we would get to go to church at other places. There was a noticeable difference of the conduct of their members though because these were not the church of Christ, they were various denominations.

In the process of time, as the girls and I began to get older, we got the idea that it was all right to go into other people's homes while they weren't home and take things we liked as long as we didn't get caught. (Mom had quit working and had started drawing a welfare check and food stamps about this time.) On one occasion, we went into someone's home and came away with some jewelry and a bag of fireworks. We played with the jewelry and ended up throwing it out into an open field and began exploding the fireworks. I guess this was what got us caught because we were taken away from home and placed in foster care for a while.

Not much had changed when we were finally allowed to return home, the old man's drinking and abuse were still present.

At school I had begun hanging around with a kid, whose mother was a marijuana dealer. I think I was eleven years of age at this time. This kid became my only friend and he would bring joints to school so we could smoke after school was out. I also spent a lot of time at his house getting high. This was my first introduction in the use of illegal drugs.

I found that when I used the marijuana that I didn't think a lot about all the problems that awaited me, at home and at school. It was an avenue of escape for me and as the years went by I became more attached to the substance. Eventually, as I got older I fell in with the pot-smoking crowd in Jr. High and High School. I felt accepted by this crowd and started adding other forms of drugs to my agenda. Alcohol was a big thing among my pot-smoking peers and so was methamphetamine. I used some of all three.

There came a point in time when my older sister's future husband came into our lives. After some time, we all moved into his house. This is when my younger sister began having problems of her own and ran away at the age of fifteen to live on her own. The old man grew tired of living under another man's roof and eventually moved out. I too decided to try and make my own way.

I worked at various jobs but was never able to hold one for any length of time due to my drinking problem, which had increased in a short period of time. These were my teen years and it was at this stage that I was introduced to crack cocaine.

Crack became my drug of choice because it was a highly addictive substance. It was also expensive. Many were the time I could go through a couple of hundred dollars in a night. Sometimes when the urge to use the drug came upon me, I didn't have the money to supply my need, I would resort to my old pattern of stealing to get what I needed to buy my drugs.

In the beginning I would shop lift or sell material under the table from the lumberyard where I was employed. Soon I moved up to breaking into businesses. Things got really bad as I entered my early twenties. Crack cocaine had become, what I thought, was a necessity. My habit had grown until I was now spending $300 to $400 each time I went to purchase the drug. When it got to the point I didn't have the money to buy the drug, I committed my first armed robbery.

On that day I had used up what little money I had smoking crack. When the money was gone, I felt that I hadn't subjected my body to a sufficient amount, so I turned it over and over in my head how I could come up with some more cash but came up with nothing. I was at a fellow's house at this time, where I was smoking the cocaine, and noticed he had a plastic handgun. I borrowed the gun and set out walking through town, passing businesses and looking them over. Soon I found a Pizza establishment and made my mind that here was where I would get myself some cash. I entered the establishment and waited until the cashier had waited on what customers were paying their bills, then I approached the counter and, placing the gun on the counter with a hand over it to conceal it, told the female cashier to open the register and give me the cash. I was arrested two days later and booked into the county jail where I spent nine months before I received my first prison sentence of 15 years.

During those nine months, I began doing Bible correspondence courses and when I arrived at my new home in prison I started going to church services. I felt that I was doing good and getting myself together. After 18 months of prison I was released on parole. I went to work immediately in Oklahoma City but eventually decided I wanted to go back to my hometown of _____. I did the paper work with my parole officer and moved back home after spending two months in OKC. I found a job for a building maintenance company and was promoted to supervisor my second month with the company. The pay was good and I found that I had plenty of extra money to spend. This fact and me being back in my old environment, soon offered the opportunity to smoke crack cocaine once again and I took it gradually. Eventually I was back using just as much of the drug as I had been before I was arrested. I was again stealing from the job, but got caught and was fired. I managed to find another job and continued using my drug.

Soon, though money began again to become scarce and I resorted to my old crime pattern and held up some convenience stores for cash. I told myself I would be smarter this time and wouldn't get caught. I robbed three stores consecutively in one night and one on another night. The night I robbed the three stores I just pretended I had a weapon, but I used the toy gun for the fourth robbery.

I wasn't as smart as I had thought I was because shortly afterward I was arrested again and booked into jail to await sentencing on my new charges. I received three twenty year sentences, run concurrently for the first three robberies, and a detainer was placed on my record for the fourth because I hadn't at the time admitted to that charge. I was then sent back to prison to finish my first fifteen-year sentence before the new one would start. This time I was sent to higher security facility than I had been on the first occasion.

During my stay in the county jail I

had again picked up a Bible and started studying. When I arrived at Stringtown, home of Mack Alford Correctional Center, I continued my studies and began to seek out where and when a church of Christ service was held. My childhood, some of my teen years and my adult years, combined with some study of God's word had led me to see that among the various denominations I had been exposed to, there was never any clear or concise pattern of teaching which fell in line with the teaching of the Bible. When I had finally come "full circle" in my life, as I like to call it, I had found that what I understood from God's word was being taught only among the people of the church of Christ.

I went to the chaplain's office to enquire about the church and baptism. The first person the chaplain sent me to was a man who I would later come to admire and respect by the name of _____ "_____" _____. I talked with _____ and told him my desire to be immersed into Christ and he in turn introduced me to Ralph Hunter. Ralph and I talked for a long period of time and soon after that conversation he baptized me into my Lord and Savior.

Ralph became a real help to me during my spiritual infancy and soon had me set up and taking correspondence courses with a school of preaching. His efforts supplied me with something that had been lacking during my first attempt to walk each day as a Christian when incarcerated the first time. That something was a continued interest in my growth, a hands-on approach which provided me with a moral support I needed to get through difficulties and move forward in the confidence that, unlike my earlier years, I had been often left to defend for myself.

Over the past years, I have been blessed to have had the benefit of gaining scriptural knowledge from many great men of God because of my association with Ralph Hunter, for which I am eternally grateful. Ralph has supplied me with a role model who I can look up to and learn from him. This is something I never had growing up, other that the short time we kids spent around Russell Schoof and his wife. Consequently, Russell came back into my life a few years back and has also been a role model and source of encouragement for me. I am indebted to both these individuals for introducing me, more than ever before, to Jesus Christ my Lord through lives they have led and the examples they have laid before me."

The following is taken from a published book an inmate has written and has granted written permission for me to use:

"As a first grader in _____, Arkansas, I was busy making memories, memories of running barefoot in the summer rain, playing baseball during recess, riding my bicycle to the store for Mother's can of Sweet Garrett Snuff. But there were also memories of crying myself to sleep, of terror beyond what a child can articulate. Endless, unavoidable, random terror ....

Weekends began innocently; in fact, Saturday's were special. I took my beloved baseball glove off my bike handles and rubbed it tenderly with my thumb, feeling the warmth and resilience as I waited for Dad to come out of the house and say 'Let's go'. I think I lived for baseball, nothing else mattered. I was seven and a budding Pee Wee leaguer. Dad was the coach, a dubious distinction for the City Marshall. Our front yard was so big

"Everyone sat quietly at our meal, careful not to rile him. Any word at all, in affection or jest, could set off a chain of events that might find one or more of us sobbing, bruised, beaten. We finished our Saturday fried chicken in silence, waiting for him to be filled and leave the table. With any luck, Saturday night might be bearable."

Dad had made it into a baseball diamond, where I often ran from base to base, fantasizing that I was Babe Ruth.

I decided to sit in the Pontiac to wait for him. He finally came out and joined me in the car, sober and eager. I smiled in anticipation of the game. Once again Dad reminded me that I was not to swing the bat. 'Don't try to hit the ball,' he said, 'you'll just strike out. Let 'em walk you to first, and then you can steal your way home.' What an ironic phrase for a Pee Wee kid too short for pitchers to strike out.

So, I followed his advice and on that particular Saturday made a score for the _____ Pee Wee League team. After the game, he treated the team to Cokes at the drug [store] on Main Street. When we got home, I stayed outside to ride my bike, and he went inside to hit the booze.

By dinnertime he was drunk. Everyone sat quietly at our meal, careful not to rile him. Any word at all, in affection or jest, could set off a chain of events that might find one or more of us sobbing, bruised, beaten. We finished our Saturday fried chicken in silence, waiting for him to be filled and leave the table. With any luck, Saturday night might be bearable.

But not Sunday. Sunday morning held the worst terror of all. It was on these mornings that my dad would take his fighting rooster to the country and there, in a run-down barn, he and other men would fight their roosters to the death. What made Sunday mornings a terror for me was that Dad would try to make me catch his roosters for him.

The roosters were kept in a long chicken-wire cage, and he needed me, or my sister B_____ A__ , to go into the cages and catch those monsters my hand. I was scared to death of those roosters, scared of the long, sharp spurs which I had seen kill other roosters. B_____ A__ didn't seem to mind this activity so much; in fact, she seemed to enjoy it. But to me it was a nightmare.

I often tried to hide on those Sunday mornings when Dad was drunk, but he always managed to find me, and after many tears and screams, he would force me into a cage. It didn't matter to him that I was afraid of the roosters. Instead, he screamed at me to stop being a crybaby. A son of his must be tough.

Sometimes my mother would try to stop him from putting me into the cage, and if he wasn't too drunk, he'd throw me into her arm and tell her to get me out of his sight. But when he was really drunk, he would slap mother and tell her to get into the house and let him make a man out of his son. My fear of those roosters got me a lot of beatings from Dad, but they were only one of the terrors of my childhood.

......

I was born in _____, September 30, 19--. When I was about six months old, my family moved to the small country town of _____, Arkansas, where my father had been appointed City Marshall. My mother was twenty-two years younger than my father, who was a very jealous man. My entire childhood is packed with memories of the constant fights between my parents.

I learned as a very young child not to come between my parents when Dad was in one of his drunken moods. I had seen him mistreat and beat my mother when he was drunk, not to mention beating me and my sister. One night after I had already gone to bed, I was awakened by the sound of my mother's crying and the loud curses of my father. I could hear what sounded like Dad hitting Mom, and I lay there crying. A hatred for the man who mistreated all of us began to grow within me. I couldn't stand the sound of Mom's crying so I got up from my bed, scared and shaking, knowing I had to try to help her just as she had always tried to help me.

When I opened the door to my parents' bedroom, my mother was lying on the floor, her face bloody. My father was standing over her, his fists raised in anger, curses raging out of his mouth, his body trembling with the violence which was destroying our family and our peace. I ran to Dad, threw my arms around his legs, and with tears streaming down my checks, I begged him to stop hitting Mom. As if swatting a fly, he swung one of his big hands against the side of my face, knocking me from around his legs. Then he kicked me in the side. He screamed at me to get _____ back to my room and never come into their room again.

I went out of that room as if I had been shot from a cannon, and never again did I get between my parents when they were fighting.

......

One Saturday morning in the summer of 1955, when I was just seven, I witnessed an act of violence by my father, and act so inhumane that it warped my mind and soul for the next 25 years. This act of violence painted a picture of power upon my memory, and carved fear and hatred into my heart for those men who wore a badge and carried a gun in the name of law and order.

On that particular morning, as we sat eating breakfast, there was a knock on our door. My mother got up to answer the door, and the next thing we heard was her screaming. Standing there in our kitchen door was our black maid, Nell, and she was covered in blood. I sat in horror as my father got up and led N___ into our kitchen. N___ told my father that her husband had come home that morning drunk and beat her up. When she threatened to come tell my father, he pulled out a razor and tried to kill her. ...... My father told her not to worry, he would make sure that her husband would never bother her again. ......

......

I watched as my father went into the bedroom to get his gun, and when he returned with it there was fire in his eyes. ...... As my father left our house, something within me pulled at me to follow him.

I knew a shortcut to N___'s house, ... so, I left mother and B_____ A__ to look after N___, and I headed toward N___'s house. ...... I arrived a minute or so before my father showed up in his patrol car. I stood across the street behind a tree, knowing that if my father saw me it would mean a whipping. ......

......

As my father pulled up in the front of the house, N___'s husband recognized and called to him. My father stepped from his patrol car, and as he stepped into the front yard he pulled his gun from his holster.

As if in a dream, I watched what happened next. I hadn't noticed it before, but N___'s husband had a razor in his hand and there was blood all over his bare chest. Father ordered him to put down the razor and come along to jail. The man mumbled something I couldn't understand, but he made no move toward my father.

Without another word, my father brought up his gun. Then as if thunder, exploded, fire shot from the barrel of the gun. My eyes raced for the black man, reaching him just in time to see him knocked against the front of the house by the power of the bullet as it struck him in the chest. ...... Twice more the gun in my father's hand exploded, shooting forth flames and burning lead; and each time the gun exploded, I could hear the smack of it against the man's chest.

There were people all around me, black faces showing fear at what they had just seen, yet knowing that they

> could not change what had happened.
> I walked from that bloody porch, my
> eyes of death, bearing within me a
> hatred for the man I called Father. As
> I walked home to face this man I had
> seen shoot down another being,
> something inside me knew that never
> would I really go back home again – I
> was simply going to a house."

It was not only fathers that were not good role models, but mothers as well. Hear the words of a 30-year-old woman, some were written and some oral. She first wrote me after talking with some other female inmates at a county jail that were taking Bible Correspondence courses that we supplied. Her first note that she sent with one of the ladies that was taking the courses contained the following message.

> "My name is "Nellie Cook" and I
> was wanting to know if you would
> pray for me. I'm in jail for drug's,
> but I'd like to tell you my story. I've
> been a prostitute since I was ten."

Through several weeks as I would visit with this young lady she made known to me, as Mr. Paul Harvey might say, "the rest of the story."

Nellie told me of a mother that had practiced the world's oldest occupation in the presence of her children, not trying to hide what she did from the two girls. Because Nellie's mother was also a drug user there were many times that food was scarce. The mother sank to the depths of 'hiring' the oldest daughter (Nellie) out to the men that had been her clients. As has already been explained in Nellie's letter, she was only 10 years old. It was not long before the mother abandoned the girls so Nellie has lived on the street for the past 20 years. Her letter went on to say:

> "I was wondering if your church
> would pray for me Sunday, I need all

the help I can get to make this new
chance in life. Also, can you send me
a book to read to get to know and
understand God better. I have a
Bible but don't understand how they
talk in it." (She had only a fourth-
grade education. *rdh*)

When I asked if she knew where her mother was, or her
father she replied that after her mother left when she was 11 or 12
she had never heard from or about her since. As for the father, she
said she had no idea who he might be, for her mother had been
with many men. The real sad part of the story is that when Nellie
was sent to a half-way house she did not keep in contact with us,
so we were not able to teach her the way of the Lord more
completely, as Aquila and Priscilla are recorded of doing with
Apollos in the 18th chapter of the book of the Acts of the Apostles.

As I related some of Nellie's story to a class of inmates at
another facility, one of those in the class asked if I would mind
letting him read a part of her letter, that he would like to respond
to some of the things she had said. This I did, not revealing her
true identity or where she was incarcerated. The following letter is
that which he asked me to send to her. Just as I had not revealed
to him Nellie's real name, neither did I give to her the name and
location of the young man.

"Nellie, the church in Owasso
shared some of your letter with me
and I was deeply touched by what
you wrote, mainly because I too was
a child of the streets, except I was the
one who sold drugs to many
categories of people and I'm positive
some were prostitutes such as
yourself. My street life didn't stop as
a drug dealer but also included gangs
and bad language, burglaries, and

thievery. Believe me Nellie I was chief in Satan's army. I knew there was a God but never had I truly worshipped Him. My life style as a worshiper of sin led to my being arrested in 1990 and sentenced to 56 years in prison. Just like you Nellie, being locked up forced me to look at myself in the mirror of God's word, and I became 'religious' in the county jail. I praised God and my Savior Christ everyday in the county, but when I transferred to prison I began to praise God less and less and go back to my old ways. Eventually I stopped praising God and again began to serve Satan, for it was in the ways of the world I found false pleasure and false satisfaction.

> It is not always just the fact of parents not being the kind of parents they need to be. In Bill's case we see that the civil authority had a great influence on a young boy's outlook toward life.

So, years went by and my sins multiplied. I began sleeping with women in my mind (lusting). I began having different women as my girl friends. I began having sex with all sorts of women who would visit me, not caring whether or not I got a disease.

Believe me Nellie, I understand what you are going through, but

> what I want to tell you is there is
> good news for you and it's called the
> 'GOSPEL'."

This young man went on to write a four page 'sermon', very accurate from scripture because he himself had become convinced of the truth of God's Word.

Another man I will call "Bill" (we will meet him again in chapter 5) who relates some other factors about not having the right kind of role model. It is not always just the fact of parents not being the kind of parents they need to be. In Bill's case, we see that the civil authority had a great influence on a young boy's outlook toward life.

Bill was raised in a family that was involved in 'moonshining' and the law was often in 'hot pursuit' of Bill and his family. A trap was set to capture Bill's father, and as was told by a very close friend of his, a brother in the Lord, that the trap included dynamite to stop the father's car. Because of this event Bill lost one of his parents and he became very bitter toward all law enforcement officials and as a result became a real live bank robber.

In all these cases, as sad and heart breaking as they are to our thinking, it is still true that one cannot blame someone else for our own actions. The prophet Ezekiel records the message of Jehovah with the following words; *"What mean you, that you use this proverb concerning the land of Israel, saying, the Fathers have eaten sour grapes, and the children's teeth are set on edge? As I live, saith the Lord God, you shall not have occasion any more to use this proverb in Israel. Behold all souls are mine; as the soul of the father, so also, is the soul of the son mine: the soul that sinneth, it shall die."* (Ezekiel 18:2 – 4) Continuing in the same chapter we find the words in verses 19 & 20 almost a carbon copy of that thought, presented in these words: *"Yet you say, Why? doeth not the son bear the iniquity of the father? When the son has done that which is lawful and right, and has kept all my statutes, and has done them, he shall live. The soul that sins, it shall die. The son shall not bear the iniquity of the father, neither shall the father bear the iniquity of the son: the righteousness of the righteous shall be upon him, and the wickedness of the wicked shall be upon him."*

Chapter 4

Life Without…
Being Able to Attend a Family Funeral

A teaching of Jesus, that is recorded for us in the Gospel of Luke, chapter 9 and verses 59 and 60, is where He says to a man, *"Follow me. But, he said, Lord, suffer me first to go bury my father. Jesus said unto him, let the dead bury the dead: ……"*

In working as a volunteer chaplain, I often filled in for the staff chaplain, either between chaplains or when the staff chaplain was gone on vacation or other business. In this capacity, it often fell my lot to have to inform inmates that there had been a death in their families. In the earlier years of my working as a volunteer the Oklahoma Prison system allowed inmates to attend funerals of fathers, mothers, siblings, or children. This was of course with two guards escorting the inmate, and the prisoner was 'cuffed and shackled'. In more recent years however, the rules have been changed in that an inmate might only go to the funeral home to view the body of the loved one, and that only for a few minutes with no one else present. This change came about for the safety of the escorting officers, for our society has become more violent and even at funerals there have been occasions when friends of the deceased bring weapons to funerals.

Even before these changes were made, it was at the warden's discretion as to allow an inmate to be taken to a funeral. This was based upon the nature of the crime, past conduct of the inmate, availability of staff to transport the offender, or where that funeral might be conducted. Only funerals conducted in the state were considered, and if a service was scheduled at a very remote location then the warden would refuse such a request. In some cases, the inmates themselves would choose not to attend, even if the family would make such a request, not wanting to have to go in leg shackles, belly chains, and, handcuffs.

There were some times that the families would ask that the inmate not be allowed to attend funerals, perhaps because of old disputes among family members or the shame of having others who might attend see the inmate coming in under such circumstances. One occasion I recall, the family had never revealed that the inmate was in fact incarcerated to his friends and acquaintances. To have him come for the funeral of a sister with guards and in constraints would have to be explained, and the 'secrets' that were not known until now would be very much in evidence. So, the authorities denied this inmate the right to go to the funeral.

No matter what the reason for not going, when an offender would hear that a mother, father, sibling, child, or some other relative had died it was hard to accept that they would not be at that service. Of course, we can understand that those of the 'free world' would have feelings for our loved ones, but what about those 'criminals' behind the iron bars and razor wire. Are there any feelings in these lawbreakers?

The following are words and thoughts of some with whom I have had contact, though not in person.

> "I came from a good family. My father was an engineer (now retired) and my mother was a schoolteacher. She passed away in 1998 after a long bout with cancer. I was already in prison when she became ill. That was probably the most difficult thing that I have ever experienced. I never got to say good bye to her."[2]

This young man was serving a sentence of less than ten years but the hurt was no less than had he been given a life

---

[2]Carolina Christian July/August 2002

sentence. Youthful desires had put him into the correctional system and it was there he had to come to face the reality of the cost of living a life of sin. It was not just that he was lost from the fellowship of the Lord, but now that there was now the separation from his earthly family at a time when he really felt the need to be with those that he loved so dearly

This young man has spent almost 20%

No matter what the reason for not going, when an offender would hear that a mother, father, sibling, child, or some other relative had died it was hard to accept that they would not be at that service. Of course, we can understand that those of the 'free world' would have feelings for our loved ones, but what about those 'criminals' behind the iron bars and razor wire. Are there any feelings in these lawbreakers?

of his life having to grieve alone over his mother's death.[3] Oh yes, there are people always around, but most could care less about a person having emotional feelings and cares. Their concern is to fulfill their wants and desires, not to really grieve because of someone else's loss. This flies in the very face of the Paul's admonition to the Christians in Rome when he penned the words, *"Rejoice with them that do rejoice, and weep with them that weep."* (Romans 12:15) Of course, we can't make this a blanket statement for there are some in the environment of the lawbreakers and disrespectful that can and will have a genuine feeling of concern for others.

For example, when the Federal building was bombed in Oklahoma City in 1995, a man in his 40s came to me saying that there was a group of inmates that would like to help in some small way a family that had lost a loved one in the bombing. "Gary" told me that the group had collected a commitment for something near $100.00. Two things we must keep in mind about this; one is that

---

[3]See Chapter 13 for a great lesson this young man wrote about Coping with Captivity.

inmates cannot collect money from one another (this will be explained in another chapter of this book), and the second is the reality that most inmates make less than $18.00 a month, this is what they have to buy their toiletries (soap, shampoo, tooth paste, etc.) and any items such as a soda or ice cream bar every now and then.

So, when Gary came to me, he came asking if I (through the church) would be a sponsor for the money to be sent to the two children of a lady that was killed in that event. Gary was from Tulsa and had read in the paper of these small children who had lost their mother. I told him I would ask if the warden would approve this and if so, I would see that the family would get the money. This proposal was granted and the money was sent to the Owasso church as a contribution and I took that sum to the home of the grandparents and delivered it along with the explanation of where it came from. The grandmother could hardly believe what she was hearing, and when I told her that the man that had organized the plan was doing a life sentence for taking another's life right there in Tulsa, she said something like, "He sure doesn't sound like a mean person." Gary was imprisoned when he was a teenager and after over 20 years of incarceration has changed a great deal. We shall meet and know more about him later in this book. I bring Gary to our attention just now simply to point out that a blanket statement cannot be made of all inmates.

> As I went into his cell to tell of his father's death, I wondered just how such news would affect him. Would he become angry and fly into a rage? Maybe there would be an outburst against the 'system' or even worse, ME. In as gentle a manner as I knew how I introduced myself to James and told him that though I was not a D.O.C. employee, at the moment I was acting in the chaplain's place and must pass on to him some very sad news.

One occasion I was asked to go and inform a 'stereotype criminal' that his father had died. I had seen this individual several times on the yard and in the chow hall, but had never had the opportunity to speak or meet him. Perhaps it is needful to describe the man so that you might be able to picture the scene.

"James" was a large man, one might even think of the country song about the miner that Jimmy Dean recorded about "Big Bad John". The words of that song states that John was a giant of a man, that with just one blow of his great big hand had sent a 'Louisiana man' to the promised land. James was such an individual, and not only big and muscular, but with the same kind of reputation. He was serving a life sentence for taking another's life. His body was almost completely covered with tattoos, many of them with suggestions of violence. His neck and much of his face was marked with such figures as knives, guns, and blood drops.

As I went into his cell to tell of his father's death, I wondered just how such news would affect him. Would he become angry and fly into a rage? Maybe there would be an outburst against the 'system' or even worse, ME. In as gentle a manner as I knew how I introduced myself to James and told him that though I was not a D.O.C. employee, at the moment I was acting in the chaplain's place and must pass on to him some very sad news. He looked at me for a moment as if almost stunned and said in a soft voice, "Has my Dad died?" His eyes filled with tears and he turned away so I wouldn't see, but I already had.

We need to stop the story here just for a moment and point out that in the prisons there is very much a 'peck order system'. It is just not the thing for an inmate, especially a big shot leader, to let others see him with tears in his eyes. To show this kind of weakness would soon have that individual labeled as one that could be intimidated somehow. So, one steels himself to not show emotions, no matter what the occasion.

Knowing this, then what transpired in the cell with James becomes even more meaningful. As he turned away from me to hide his emotions I spoke to him with something like these words: "James, there is no one else in this cell and I will stand with my back covering the window (a very small window where officers could look in at count times to see if all inmates were where they were supposed to be), so you may feel free to take this time to grieve if you so desire." With that, this very serious 'criminal' put his arms around my shoulders and began to shed tears unashamedly. For several minutes, he sobbed and uttered such words as if talking to his dad, "Why have I let you down?" "Why didn't I listen when you taught me right from wrong?" I did not attempt to make him break his hold around my neck, but waited until he finally dropped his massive arms to his side and wiped the tears from his face on his shirtsleeve. He turned and sat down on his bunk and began apologizing to me for his actions. I assured him there was nothing to be ashamed about and asked him if he had ever read the account in John 11 of Jesus weeping when told about his friend Lazarus' death? He replied that he never read the Bible.

After James had made the effort to be allowed to go to his father's funeral, and was denied that privilege, my thoughts were: "I wonder if he will blame me, and will I ever have opportunity to speak with him about his soul's destiny?" I never again had the opportunity to talk with him again in private about such things, but every time I would pass him on the yard and there was no one close by, he would stop for just a moment and say, "Thanks for being such a good friend," and then go on his way.

Another occasion much like the events with James, it was my lot to inform a man about the death his mother. I had never met this inmate, in fact I cannot remember of ever having seen him in the population of that facility before I was sent to him with news about his mother, though he had been there for several years. He was not an individual that would stand out to us outsiders. However, he was well known by the officers, and as I asked the officer on duty where his cell was and gave the reason for my needing to see him, the officer said to me: "Be sure to inform the shift Captain what you are doing, so we can watch him and if need be, to lock him down." The reason for this type of thinking was that sometimes bad news from family causes some inmates to react in disorderly ways. But such was not the case with "Rick". As with James, I assured him that he was free to shed his tears with no other inmate knowing what was going on in his cell nor why I had made the visit until he wanted to reveal the facts. Unlike the case with James, Rick was eligible to attend that funeral if he so desired, but I do not remember if he took advantage of that privilege.

It was not many weeks later that Rick started attending our Bible study class that was conducted each week and then became almost a regular visitor with me on the yard. Soon he was attending the Sunday service that some brethren from the Southwest Ada, Oklahoma congregation conducted each week. Within a year, he obeyed the gospel and is a leader in the little congregation that meets in that facility.

Several years later the church in Owasso received a letter from Rick, part of which follows:

> "Church of Owasso, First I would like to give thanks to our Lord Jesus Christ for all the blessings I have received, not only from the Lord but also from the church there in Owasso. Thanks so very much dear friends for the love you have shown me over the years. Back in 1997 I lost my mother to a heart attack. I thought my life was over, but little did I know that it was just beginning. Ralph Hunter was the one who came and told me of her passing. This was the first time I ever met Ralph, and did my life ever change."

Just how did Rick's life change? As already stated, the staff knew Rick very well and in fact had on several occasions 'written him up' for various reasons. I might need to explain here what a 'write up' means. Just as there are rules of conduct on the outside of prison walls, such as traffic laws as we drive, rules for children in school as they are in the halls between classes or in the class room or practices that are expected of workers in the work force either for getting the job done or perhaps safety reasons. When these ordinances are violated then some form of punishment is administered. That might be anything from a mild reprimand to some sort of fine. So also, is a write up.

The rules, called 'opps' (operation procedures) cover a number of things. They range from requirements for cleanliness of personal hygiene to living area kept in order to actions of the inmate at work, recreation, toward staff, and toward other inmates. Rick through the years had been written up for among other things, gambling, doing drugs, disrespect to staff, having contraband, and bartering. He had been in the Restricted Housing Unit (DU in the language of the inmates) a number of times in the 8 to 10 years before I met him. I suppose, to put it mildly, Rick was a problem inmate!

So, when he wrote to the church stating, "......and did my life ever change." That was about as great an understatement as the passage in Matthew 4:2 when the declaration is made that Jesus hungered after going without food forty days. In the first year or so after Rick started attending all the services of the church one of the officers came to me with this question. "What did you do to Rick to change him so much?" When I responded to the officer, why he would ask such a question he said that there was just a different person that looked like Rick. Now they could shake down his cell all they wanted to and they never found anything, and there was always a polite response to whatever order was given him.

The other side of the coin is that not only in many cases that the prisoner cannot be with his loved ones in the times of family bereavement but there cannot be family close when ill health or death is visiting the door of one who is incarcerated.

Two important factors must be considered here. One, sometimes the family has given up on the inmate and has not even tried (perhaps for years) to visit him or her while they are incarcerated, let alone when they are ill. Many times, the prisoner knows of the seriousness of the ailment and longs for the family to have some contact but none is forthcoming even if the family would be allowed. The second factor that comes into play is there are times when sudden illnesses occur and even death takes place unexpectedly.

Such was the situation with "Guy", age about 35 years old. I had known Guy for several years and he came to our Bible classes on a regular basis. He had become very comfortable being around me, and talked openly with me about his past life and case. Some of the things he shared with me were about his married (several times) life and about how one of those wives had been killed in the tornado that ripped through Oklahoma City. Guy told me how that because of his crime, he had no contact with any family member, and in fact when he had tried to write a sister, his letter had been returned which led to him being placed in solitary confinement for three weeks. (There was a court order that he should have no contact with any family member and punishment for violation was time in DU.)

The day Guy was let out of DU we had a long study together, and much of the time was dealing with the question of marriage and divorce. I remember well the conversation and some of the final thoughts were, that if he ever was released that by God's law he would never have the right to be married. The next day when I came onto the yard the officer at the gate told me that Guy had died in his bunk that night. When contact was made with his family about what kind of funeral arrangements should be made, the reply was for the state to bury him in what is known in the language of the prison, 'Peckerwood Hill', a place in the Oklahoma Correctional facility at McAlester where bodies of unclaimed inmates are buried.

I will take just a moment here to share with you, a note that I received after getting home the week Guy died.

> "Mr. Ralph Hunter
> church of Christ
>
> Dear Ralph, Greetings.
> This letter is to inform you that I look forward to our bible study tomorrow night. I hope to see you there.
> Sincerely,
> Guy W   #222222"

In the past, in the case of terminal illness of an immediate family member, an inmate could in some instances get an 'emergency medical pass'. This has now been discontinued because of security considerations. But I have never known of a situation in which family could not be in contact with an inmate in the hospital. However, such was the case as I record it in the next events.

A man we shall call "Robert" suffered heart trouble, and was placed in the hospital in Oklahoma City to undergo open heart surgery. While in the hospital he was not allowed to have any visitors, even volunteers such as myself. In the hospital, there is a secured ward, with at least two officers at the entrance to the ward and always an officer at the door of the room in which the inmate recuperates. When I was informed that Robert had been taken to Oklahoma City for surgery as I arrived at the facility for our regularly scheduled Bible study, I made plans to go there the next day (this was two days after the surgery) to visit with him. Upon arrival, I presented my 'badge' that allowed me to go into any (D.O.C.) correctional facility in the state with full feeling that I could visit this brother at his hospital bedside. Such was not the case, so I learned another lesson about jail/prison evangelism. Even sickness does not allow the volunteer to go where he feels he is needed.

Several years after the forgoing episode, I did encounter an event that rather shocked me. One that it seemed to me that I would never have been allowed to be a part. At the Mack Alford C.C. near Atoka, Oklahoma the railroad track runs in front of the facility just across the Highway. Some of the inmates of the Minimum-Security part of the facility are taken across the railroad to work on the 'farm'. After lunch one afternoon, as the crew was being taken back, the officer that was driving for some reason failed to stop at the R/R crossing and was struck by a train. The officer and one of the inmates were killed in the wreck. The inmate that was killed was a young man that had been attending our Bible class for a number of weeks, and had just been baptized two weeks prior. "Bill" had asked, just a few days before his death, that I write his wife to encourage her to study the same Bible Courses that he had been going through.

The warden called me at my home and asked (I think the inmate's wife had requested) that I come to conduct the funeral at the facility. My answer to the warden was in the affirmative and I was allowed to conduct that service in the visiting room. Along with the family members there were in attendance many of the inmates of that yard. The small congregation that made up the church there had a great part in the service, one brother leading the group in a song, another leading a prayer, and a couple of others acting as casket bearers. Bill was then taken to his hometown for burial.

Though this was the only funeral that I had any part, being conducted in the facility itself, I was allowed by the wardens of two other facilities to be with the inmates at the funerals of their loved ones. In these cases, (one serving a life sentence for murder and the other for a very long sentence) the inmate could not be seated with any family member or friends, only the two security guards that were assigned to transport the inmate to the funeral. One of the occasions was a grandmother that had raised the inmate.[4] The other was a funeral for the inmate's wife. However, the two wardens granted these two inmates their request that I could be with them for 'comfort', being seated next to the guards. Keep in mind the prisoners were in 'restraints', (cuffs, black boxes, shackles) at all times and the two officers, one on either side. The first of these funerals was a graveside service and the second in a funeral home.

In additions to these three funerals, I was asked by two other inmates to conduct services for family members: neither of these men were permitted to be in attendance for these services. However, both men asked that I give them copies of the presentation made at those services. A chaplain for one of those facilities allowed me to bring him a recording of the service (songs, prayers, and sermon) and he played it for the inmate. That recording was returned to me after only the inmate heard it in the chaplain's office.

---

[4]The inmate was 25 to 30 years old.

Chapter 5

Life Without…
Taking Time to Know the Bible

So many times the statement: "By being put into prison was an event that perhaps saved my life, for I never took the time to study the Bible while on the street," or something like that has been spoken to me. More than one individual put it in these words, "Perhaps coming to prison saved my life, for I didn't take time to see how important the Word of God was."

One does not have to look far in the scriptures to find a man who made a similar statement. In Acts 24 and verse 25, governor Felix is recorded as saying, *"Go thy way for this time; when I have a convenient season, I will call for thee."* As

> More than one individual put it in these words, "Perhaps coming to prison saved my life, for I didn't take time to see how important the Word of God was."

far as we are told in the scriptures, there never was a convenient season for Felix and if that was the case he would have died in his sin as we would understand from John 8:*24 "I said therefore unto you, that ye shall die in your sins: for if ye believe not that I am he, ye shall die in your sins."* Unfortunately, we find many who have shared that same concept of Felix, just waiting for a convenient season, but there just does not seem to be that convenient season to have time to hear or study the Word of the Lord. Thus, when the steel bar door is shut behind them, and there is only the hopeless feeling that all is lost, now they take time to open the Bible. Some might open it just to look for a way out of jail, but some might look into it for a way out of the sin that is in their life.

The following are just a few of the comments that have come my way, either by verbal conversation or by written page, but all saying very much the same thing.

"Chuck" wrote:

> "I have always believed that God was my Creator and the Father of the world. I also was brought up believing that God sent His only son to die in order to forgive us humans of our sins. I was never a regular church going person. I didn't see the need for it. (Didn't take the time to know. *rdh*) When I came to prison I recognized my need to learn about and follow God. I looked for the way to learn this way of living. I was given a lot of literature, magazines and even a Bible. But I still did not know what to do with it. I didn't feel any comfort with the knowledge that was put in my possession. ......"

Chuck goes on to declare that when one took the time to answer his questions, as he states:

> "......it answers based on a specific book, chapter and verse out of the Bible" was easy for him to understand. "at that time, I didn't understand what this was going to mean to my life. ...... I have found a great amount of comfort and peace

with myself, and relief from the situation I have put myself in. But this comfort only came to me when I was baptized and accepted as a part of the body of Christ at Owasso and other places. So, to all my brothers and sisters in the churches of Christ, I thank you."

As I mentioned in the preface section of this book, I was preaching for the church of Christ in Collinsville, Oklahoma when I started going into the county jail on a regular basis. The church in Collinsville had become somewhat well know because of a lawsuit that had been brought against her that was reported by the news media throughout the county, in fact in much of the world. The church received a great amount of correspondence from all across the country. There were letters from sister congregations and other religious groups from far and wide. Among those letters was one from a little congregation that met inside the confines of the _____, Oklahoma Federal Correctional Center. It was through the influence of one of the men from this group that was a strong motivation that moved me toward prison evangelism.

This little group of Christians had their start with a convicted bank robber who had been transferred from a federal facility in a southern state. This inmate told me many times (after his release from prison) of his deeds before going to prison, and of how he did not take any time to study the Word of God, in fact as a youngster he had become so disillusioned with religion that he wanted nothing to do with it. In an earlier chapter (Life Without... A Proper Role Model) we were introduced to this man and how he influenced hundreds of souls to study the Word of God to the point of obedience to the gospel. But for now, I want to focus on the fact he spent many years having no interest in the Word of God, but through the desire of another inmate he began to take some time to read and study this book that we know of as 'The Bible'.

It is a thrilling story of how this man we shall call "Bruce", by his own words 'a mean man', could not stand to see and hear the sexual abuse that some inmates were putting on another young inmate. One night, shortly after his arrest, Bruce heard the violence of an attack on a youngster in a cell near his. The pleading from the young man to those that were perpetrating this vile act to please stop, and then the cries and sobbing that followed the attack fell on the ears of Bruce. He could do nothing to stop that event, being in a different cell. But a short time later, when another young man was brought into that same area and the same scheme was made known to Bruce, he asked the jailer if the youngster could be placed in the tank where he was. That request was granted. When some inmates began to threaten the young man, Bruce stood in front of him and said, "You will have to whip me before you touch him."

It needs to be known that Bruce was by no means a 'frail 97 -pound weakling' and as a result the inmates that were planning the attack backed away from carrying out their plans. Let me here pass on to you something Bruce told me after he was released from prison. Bruce said to me, "Many people thought I must have had some 'CHRISTIANITY' in me before I came to know the truth. Perhaps thinking, I never was seen not fully dressed, that I must have been very modest! Not so, it was just that I always wore a jacket or suit coat to cover the .45 under my arm. I was mean!"

The young man that Bruce befriended could not read, and soon asked Bruce if he would help him to read the Bible. This he was willing to do even though he had no interest in studying it for himself. As the days passed these two new friends, one listening and the other reading, began to learn truths from the scriptures that would change not only their lives, but many more men and women over the next 20 or so years. Now, the man that had not taken time for some 30 years to study God's Word turned not only into a student of that Word but also a great teacher of it. In the federal facility where he was incarcerated he began to make contact with Christians on the outside, and with another bank robber, they wrote several congregations searching for truth. They asked questions like, "What is your understanding of the inspiration of the Bible?" and "What is the church?"

These two 'BANK ROBBERS' were instrumental in starting the congregation of the Lord's church in the Federal Correctional Institution located in El Reno, Oklahoma. The following is some of the article written by a man we shall know as "Rob", which was published in the *Gospel Advocate* in a January issue of that publication, with names of individuals changed (as I have not used real names of inmates throughout this book.) But, every detail mentioned is an exact quotation from that letter. I thank the editor of the *Gospel Advocate* for allowing me to use this material!

"The beginnings of the congregation at F.C.I. _____, were in a _____ jail cell in 1978. A bank robber was apprehended and jailed for the first time in his life.

With the realization that he was finally in a situation he could not control or escape, Bruce tried to adjust to the environment.

A fellow prisoner requested help from him in understanding the Bible. Bruce, an educated man, agreed to help with the King James Version which is so hard for most imprisoned men to read. (They are usually handicapped by reading difficulties.) Bruce never suspected that he would begin to see the truth unfold from the pages of the famous book.

As the days and weeks went by, other prisoners in the jail began to listen as Bruce described what he was seeing in the Word. When the plan of salvation became evident, every means of being immersed inside the jail building was investigated by those prisoners who desired to become Christians. It soon became clear that the then present circumstances would not allow scriptural obedience to take place.

A prayer went up from those men, asking for a chance to be buried with their Lord in baptism. The next day a preacher came to visit. It seemed he had been trying to get permission for a visit inside the jail. That day, the same sheriff who had denied the preacher's request for so long, suddenly said yes.

Meeting Bruce and the searching men in the old jail, the preacher soon learned of their desire to be baptized. The preacher left, quickly reentering the jail with an inflatable child's wading pool that had been in the trunk of his car only a day or two.

The preacher made arrangements with the jail staff and soon many men were completing the first steps of obedience to become Christians.

In 1979 Bruce arrived at FCI _____, Oklahoma, a Federal prison. During the following 18 months, he converted five men who were baptized into Christ. At the end of that time none of these new Christians had an answer to the question, "Do we have any brethren in the free world?" Of all different "religions" represented in this FCI chapel facility, not one new testament Christian from the free world was coming here in 1979, 1980, or 1981. Denominational bands, choirs, seminars, and meetings were and still are, pouring in here at such a rate it takes two to three months notice to schedule a program for the chapel facility.

In February of 1981, I arrived here, a convicted bank robber like Bruce. I had already engaged in a search for information about a man-god whose true existence I had accepted on the eve of 1981. After sampling every available 'Bible study' class in the FCI chapel, and coming up hungry of spirit, I began studying in private with Bruce and two other inmates, Roger G. and Albert B. Together we studied the word of God in a fashion not allowed by other groups. We took each Bible verse slowly, turning it in our minds to every possible angle for inspection. On several occasions we spent hours studying just a few verses. Bruce remained silent as much as possible, waiting to see if we would arrive at the same conclusion as he himself had months before.

We began to see a picture of a church that was radically foreign to what three of our group had ever heard of on the streets. Bruce was raised a Baptist, Roger had been a member of the Assemblies of God, and I had been raised Methodist. Albert B. had been raised in a family that assembled with a group that called themselves a congregation of the churches of Christ.

Albert would occasionally tell us that what we were seeing in the Bible sounded like the church he remembered from his childhood. His memories were vague so none of us were certain this group wasn't just another denomination.

The months from March – July of 1981 were used by us for heavy study (30 to 40 hours per week, while holding 40 hour a week jobs. *rdh*) by each man in pursuing knowledge on the basic structure of the church. ...... After becoming convinced of the plan of salvation, Albert B. was baptized. I soon followed. This was in May of 1981. Roger G. would later obey the Gospel. Other men to whom we related our learning began to study and to respond. As of this writing, December 1983, 86 men have been baptized in this prison, 81 of these since May of 1981.

Our brother Albert B. continued to recall more childhood memories and in July of 1981 we began to wonder if there was a chance that his parents were in fact, Christians who were worshiping with a scriptural body of believers. We composed and mailed a letter to the elders of the Ridgewood church of Christ, Beaumont, Texas, where Albert's parents assembled. The letter included 20 questions concerning the basic structure of the church Christ died for. When the answer came two weeks later, we found it a carbon copy of what we ourselves were professing."

Bible class at Strimetown ! · ' ·

The article in the *Gospel Advocate* continues and chronicles the work and efforts of several of those who were converted in FCI, _____. One Hispanic brother who completed his sentence, is now preaching the Gospel to incarcerated men in Mexican jails. Another, from Barranquilla, Columbia plans to establish a congregation of the Lord's church in his home since there is not a congregation in that city.

The brother who wrote the article, as well as the 'other bank robber' mentioned, have been dear and close friends of mine, for many years. The author, taught his mother who has also been a treasured friend of mine, is now living in the Tulsa area, and is a member of a congregation in a community close by.

Jess Dunn -
Taft, OK

LARC Lexington 1987

Chapter 6

Life Without...
A Feeling of Remorse for My Sins

What would make it easy for one to not have any remorse for the wrong that he has done? There are many answers I suppose, but one of the more prevalent is **[1]** that someone else's transgressions are much worse than mine so therefore it somehow justifies me for doing what I did. This is the attitude we read about in Luke 18:9 –11. *"And He spake this parable unto certain which trusted in themselves that they were more righteous, and despised others: Two men went up into the temple to pray; the one a Pharisee, and the other a publican. The Pharisee stood and prayed thus with himself, God, I thank thee, that I am not as other men are, extortioners, unjust, adulterers, or even as this publican."*

"George", a young man, I would guess to be about 25 years old, was sitting across the desk from me as we looked into the scriptures concerning some subject that I don't even remember. What I do remember is that as we talked, another young man came into the room and George got up to leave so I suggested to the man that had just come in to let me have a few more minutes with the first individual. The second fellow was very polite and

I must say here that I never made it a practice in all the years I spent in jail/prison evangelism of asking anyone with whom I studied, why, or for how long, they were incarcerated.

apologized for interrupting our conversation and when he had gone out and closed the door, George sat back down. My expression I supposed asked the question even before the words came from my mouth. "Why did you not want to continue our conversation when Bob came in? We were only talking about the scriptures." His answer was something like this, "I don't want to be around people like him." As our conversation continued, George told me that "Bob" was a convicted sex offender, what is known in prison talk as, "a baby raper". I Corinthians 6:9 – 11!!!!

I must say here that I never made it a practice in all the years I spent in jail/prison evangelism of asking anyone with whom I studied, why, or for how long, they were incarcerated. There are at least two reasons for this. One is that we might become judgmental as to whom we want to try and teach and the other is the individual we approach might feel that we are more interested in what his or her crime might be rather than just to teach them about the Lord. It must be understood that sin of any kind was not 'whitewashed' in the scriptures, and neither did we. Paul states in II Corinthians 5:10, *"For we must all appear before the judgment seat of Christ; that every one may receive the things done in his body, according to that he hath done, whether it be good or bad."* Thus, to those that were incarcerated for crimes such as Bob's were taught that their lives must be filled with repentance just as any other 'convict'.

George, what are you saying about Bob? Is your transgression, whatever it might be, any less hideous before God than his? If that is the case, we would have to find in the scriptures sins categorized and then look to see if there is one kind of repentance for one sin and another kind of repentance for a more grievous one. I presented the apostle Paul's writing to Timothy (*"Christ came into the world to sinners, of whom I am chief."* I Timothy 1:15) to him. When I brought this to George's attention his defense was something like: "I just don't think that I have done anything as bad as a 'baby raper', and that God would look with more disgust at someone who would do something like that. All I can say is I'm glad I'm not like that."

There were at least two faulty points of reasoning in George's response, and I have no way of knowing how much of an impact of what I said to him made, but this is basically the remainder of our conversation. I must add that there were never any heated or unkind words in our entire visit, and George left with no hard feelings as far as I could tell. His first point of reasoning I pointed out to him was the, 'I think' logic he started with. As we had been talking about, and studying the scriptures when Bob came in, I asked George to turn in his Bible to Isaiah chapter 55 and read for me verses 8 & 9 (*"For my thoughts are not your thoughts, neither are your ways my ways, saith the Lord. For as the heavens are higher than the earth, so are my ways higher than your ways, and my thoughts than your thoughts."*) Our conversation continued as I asked him, "You said you just didn't think you have done anything as bad as Bob, are you speaking as one that has the same thinking as the Lord or is this the Lord's thoughts?"

I then asked him to turn to the story of Naaman the leper in II Kings 5 and read it for me. He looked a little puzzled as he looked at the first few lines as if to say, "What has this got to do with me?" but he respectfully read the first 10 verses of the event. When he began to read verse eleven his expression changed some-what as he read, "......, *and said, Behold I thought,......*" After George had finished reading through the eleventh verse I asked him if he thought Naaman's thoughts were the Lord's thoughts. George's answer, "I hadn't thought about that, but I still don't want to be around that kind of person."

The second point I addressed about George's reasoning was: when Christ taught His disciples about praying He said to them; *"And when you pray, ... And forgive us our debts, as we forgive our debtors."* (Matthew 6:5 – 12) I asked George if he would like to be forgiven by the Lord for all that he had been guilty of in his life, and he answered, "I sure would."

According to the writings of inspired men, for one to have forgiveness of our transgressions we must first be willing to for-give others. One of the things Jesus taught about prayer, recorded for us in Matthew 6:12, was to ask forgiveness as one is willing to forgive others. *"And forgive us our debts, as we forgive our debt-ors."* Again, in Matthew the 18th chapter verses 21 through 35 our Lord taught a strong lesson about the expectation of forgiveness only after being ready to forgive. *"Then came Peter to Him, and said, Lord, how oft shall my brother sin against me, and I forgive him? till seven times? Jesus saith unto him, I say not unto thee, until seven times: but, until seventy times seven. Therefore the kingdom of heaven is likened unto a certain king, which would take account of his servants. And when he had begun to reckon, one was brought unto him, which owed him ten thousand talents. But forasmuch as he had not the ability to pay, his lord command-ed him to be sold, and his wife, and his children, and all that he had, and payment to be made. The servant therefore fell down, and worshipped him, saying, Lord have patience with me, and I will pay thee all. Then the lord of that servant was moved with compassion, and loosed him, and forgave him the debt. But the same servant went out, and found one of his fellow servants, which owed him an hundred pence: and he laid hands on him, and took him by the throat, saying, Pay me that thou owest. And his fellow servant fell down at his feet, and besought, saying, Have patience with me, and I will pay thee all. And he would not: but went and cast him into prison, till he should pay the debt."*

The first thought that came into my mind as George set these reasoning's before me was the writing of the apostle Peter in his first letter, saying in 4:11, *"If any man speak, let him speak as the oracles of God;"*, and in the third chapter speaking God's ora-cles, writes *"...... Sanctify the Lord God in your hearts: and be ready always to give an answer to every man that asketh you a reason of the hope that is in you with meekness and fear:"* (3:15) When I expressed these thoughts to him and asked him if there was a Bible answer to justify his feelings about Bob (and others who had the same type charge) he shrugged and said, "I don't guess so." And with that he excused himself and left, passing Bob standing outside the door without acknowledging his presence. I wish I could tell you that there were other occasions that I had a chance to talk and study with George, but that is not the case.

Turning the clock, (or we might say 'the calendar'), in fast forward mode about ten years; we shall meet a man (may we know him as, "Roland") that had been convicted of the crime that George had expressed he wanted nothing to do with such a person.

Roland was convicted and given a sentence of 25 years; in the terms of convicts, 'two tens and a five, running wild'. Mean-ing that Roland would have to do one sentence of ten years and then begin serving the next ten-year sentence before starting the five-year sentence. To those unfamiliar with laws dealing with prison sentences, a convicted individual can 'earn' time reduction of that sentence by 'good time'. Often, we hear the expression, 'perfect prisoner', one who causes no problems and always obeys all the rules. This would well define Roland. In the twelve years I knew and had him as a student, he never had a 'WRITE UP', and was commended many times by his supervisors (staff or officers) for doing more than was expected or required. A prisoner can 'earn' level 2 after 90 days with no write ups, then gain level 3 after another 90 days, and then after one year level 4. Level 2 gives a prisoner 22 days credit toward his release each month he has served those 30 days without a write up. Level 3 gives the prisoner 33 days credit for each month served (in addition to the 33 days he has served), and level 4 provides 44 days credit for the month served. Roland therefor completed his 25-year sentence in just over 12 and half years.

About a year before his release, Roland was teaching a Bible class among about a dozen men who were all serving time as sex offenders, and many were making statements such as, "I'm not guilty, or I'm no worse than Bill, Sam, Joe, or Henry." Roland responded with these words, "Am I the only guilty one in this group?" On my next visit to that unit, some three days later, several of that class came to me with the thought that Roland had opened their eyes to the need of seeing their sins instead of hiding it. Before his release, two of those in his class were buried with the Lord in baptism.

Another reason [2] for one not having remorse for his sins might be summed up by saying something like, "Johnny made me do it, it's not my fault." This next episode has this for a reason.

As I have mentioned I never asked why individuals were incarcerated, but there were times that some inmates seemed almost proud of their 'accomplishment'. One such young man began telling me his story not more than ten minutes after I met him. "William" joined in the group that I was visiting with at the TV area the first week he was on the yard of that facility and asked if he could talk with me. Thinking that he wanted to go into an area where we would have some little bit of privacy I responded by saying we could go into the chaplain's office. To my surprise, he said that it would be fine just where we were. This is a very unusual thing for an inmate to say or do, but he started telling me his story immediately.

To see this man's physical stature will give a hint about his psyche. He was a very small man, with some deformity of his arms almost appearing dwarfish. He stood about 66 inches tall, weighing not more than 130 pounds. Though small physically he did not lack in thinking ability, having above intelligence in mathematics and electronics.

As we began to talk (keeping in mind that other inmates were within hearing distance) he told me his story why he was in prison. Like many others that I came in contact in the years of prison evangelism, he had taken the life of his wife. However, unlike most of these inmates who never wanted to talk about their crimes, William not only wanted to tell the story, but seemed almost proud of 'his accomplishments'.

Working in a foreign country as a designer of electronic equipment he had met and married a girl of that nation. When they moved back to his native Oklahoma his wife withdrew herself from him both emotionally and physically. The scriptures teach of course that this is not good in a relationship: *"Let the husband render unto the wife due benevolence: and likewise also the wife unto the husband. The wife hath not power of her own body, but the husband: and likewise also the husband hath not power over his own body, but the wife. Defraud ye not one the other, except it be with consent for a time, that ye may give yourselves to fasting and prayer; and come together again, that Satan tempt ye not for your incontinency."* (I Corinthians 7:3 – 5) But he, nor his wife were directed by or cared about the Word of God.

William began to find letters addressed to his wife, written in her native language that he could not read. Taking one of these letters to a person who could translate them for him, he learned that she was sending love messages to a man she had met when she had returned home for a visit. William also learned from this letter that his wife had purchased a return ticket to her homeland and had plans to file for divorce and go to marry this man.

As William continued his conversation he became more and more detailed. I asked him, "Why are you telling all these things in front of all these other men?" and his reply to me was, "She only got what she deserved."

He continued his story telling how his wife refused his advances once again so he tied her hands above her head with a rope over a rafter in their house, and in his words, "shot her dead!" He then said that now she could not refuse his advances and "had his way with her". After burying the body in a dog pen, he prepared the pen to have cement poured according to plans that he had made the week before.

Taking the plane tickets for her return to her home country he flew to Dallas under her name, got a boarding pass from her ticket, then bought a ticket back to Tulsa under his own name. When the wife did not arrive in her native country the waiting 'boyfriend' called the home of William to see if she had left. Upon hearing this, William now contacted the police to make a missing person report.

It was not many days after this conversation that I saw William and he was almost frantic looking for a 'shank' (prison language for knife) because his cellmate was threatening him. Why? Because the story he had told me in the presence of other inmates had been spread all over the prison yard.

When William started telling me this story my

Before we come to the details about these happenings I want to make it clear that I personally never felt at any moment in all the 16 years that I went into the correctional facilities a concern for my safety. This does not mean that there could not have been something happen, but I never had any feeling of danger for my personal safety.

thoughts were that perhaps he was wanting to 'get things off his chest', to as the words of the apostle in I John 1:9 *"confess your faults......"* (Although he did not understand that in context) but that was not his intent. He was simply making his claim to fame.

How wonderful it would be to be able to say that this young man learned the gospel and repented. But alas, such is not the case to my knowledge. He was soon transferred from that prison facility to another and I have not had contact with him for more than 25 years. I did visit with his mother shortly after he was shipped, but she was very cold and not willing to reveal any information about where he was. I might add that when I asked her if she would be willing to search the Word of God with me she invited me to leave her place of business.

Two other events come to mind that indelibly stamp in my heart just how unrepentant and hardened some individual's spirits can become. Before we come to the details about these happenings I want to make it clear that I personally never felt at any moment in all the 16 years that I went into the correctional facilities a concern for my safety. This does not mean that there could not have been something happen, but I never had any feeling of danger for my personal safety.

The first of these events occurred as I was filling in for the chaplain for a week while he was on vacation. A young man that I had read about in the Tulsa newspaper, came into the office the first week he was on the yard. He had a great resemblance to a well-known TV and movie star, so much so that l made the remark to him of how much he looked like that individual. He answered me with a rather belligerent, "That's what everyone says and why I can't get away with anything."

It was just a couple of days later that I was called by the yard officer (security major) and told to immediately send every inmate to their cell, not to take time to put anything away and for the inmates to go directly to their housing. Officers would be stationed along the sidewalks and anyone not hurrying to their cells would be punished.

As my thoughts raced in my head, wondering just what had triggered such a command, the phone rang again in the office and the deputy warden said that I was to come to the leisure library as quickly as possible.

The distance between the chaplain's office and the library was not more than a hundred yards, just down a single flight of stairs and across the open yard in front of the 'chow hall'. As I ran past the chow hall I saw guards at the door, yet some inmates still seated at the tables (steel tables fastened to the floor) and was puzzled that all inmates were not 'locked down'. As I got to the doorway of the library it was plain what had happened. Officers were surrounding the door and the female librarian lay on the floor being comforted by one of the other female staff members. An inmate (the young man mentioned above, though not known at that moment) had hid himself behind a bookshelf as all other inmates had been sent out of the library for lunch. As the librarian closed and locked the door the young inmate attacked and raped her. In the attack, he had tried to kill her by beating her head against the concrete floor. After the attack, he unlocked the door and ran into the kitchen where he was assigned as a dishwasher.

The second female staff member had come as she usually did to have dinner with the librarian in the library office, and came upon the scene. As the emergency alarm was sounded, the call went out to send all inmates to their cells, with the exception of those in the chow hall where the only person that could have come from the library would be. It was not more than 15 minutes after the alarm was issued, until an ambulance was at the door of the library. The distance between the ambulance and the door of the chow hall was not more than a dozen feet, but there was not an inmate allowed near a window nor the door of the large dining area, all were ordered to stay seated at their table. The kitchen help were all told to stand in one small section of the kitchen and correctional officers watched that no one moved out of that room.

Let me insert here something that I had never seen before and never saw again in all the years I was on medium or higher security prison yards. There are always at least two 12-foot-high gates to pass through going into or out of such a facility. You do not see those two gates opened at the same time, one is opened for the vehicle or pedestrian(s) to enter the 'sally port' and when that gate is closed then the other gate is opened for exit. This is both entering into, or exiting from the facility. On this occasion both gates were opened at the same time when the ambulance approached the facility and as it left with the librarian. Several armed officers stood at the entrance. (Keep in mind that there was no movement on the yard of any inmate.)

After the ambulance had departed for the hospital, the deputy warden (the warden was not on the facility) came to me and asked that I follow the ambulance to the hospital, and to make contact with the librarian's husband to notify him of the situation. However, when we arrived at the hospital someone had already made contact with him and he was waiting.

Back to the young man involved, as I mentioned he had only been on the yard for a week or so and as is the usual case, one of the first jobs an inmate is assigned is that of a dishwasher. This young man was placed in that position, thus was near the library. I would learn that his conviction was for rape and without a penitent heart he now returned to his former thoughts and actions. But, like King David (II Samuel 11) his lusts led him to try and cover that action by attempting to murder the victim. If there is any good part of the story it would be that the librarian survived.

The second event that demonstrated to me about an unrepentant soul was a couple of years after a costly riot at one of the facilities. This came about as a result of one inmate stealing a radio from another inmate and when a confrontation took place between an inmate that had seen the first man taking the radio and the man that had stolen it. It soon ballooned into full scale riot, much of it coming from a racial cause. Several months later as I visited in a county jail I came in contact with a young man that boasted to me that he was the 'thief' that had brought about the trouble that night When I asked if he had any remorse for what followed that event his answer to me was, "Why should I?" As far as I know that young man still has that same attitude, for after that visit I never saw him again.

Let us always keep in mind the admonition spoken of by the Christ in Luke 13:3 & 5: *"I tell you, Nay; but, except ye repent, ye shall all likewise perish."* These people I have just told you about did not heed these words. DO WE?

Chapter 7

Life Without…
Self-Discipline

"I have done things that I wanted to do all my life," were the words that "Harry" said to me as I visited with him through the 'bean hole' of the steel door of the Restricted Housing Unit (RHU, in the language of the prison yard, sometimes referred to as DU) Also for the sake of most of the readers, 'the bean hole' is a 4" x 10" opening in the solid steel door of the 5' x 10' cell. (There is a very small window about eye level for officers to check on inmates several times a day.) This opening (bean hole) is covered on the outside by a steel plate that can be dropped open only from the outside for a meal tray to be passed through at mealtime for the inmate. The bean hole is just above knee high, so to talk with one in 'the hole' requires almost one to sit on the floor or spend a lot of time bending over.

In this room (cell), is a steel shelf where a 3" mattress is given for a bed and only one army type blanket, a toilet, and a hand basin. My conversations with inmates in this situation is through the bean hole. Harry had sent a 'request of staff' to the chaplain's office for me to come and visit with him. I had known and had occasions to speak to him many times on the yard, but it had never been much more than a short greeting and a friendly hello. So, when the chaplain gave me the message I was very surprised.

It was not a new thing for this inmate to be in DU, in fact I had known of at least three other times that he had been in this situation after I had known him, and perhaps many other times on other yards. As I began my conversation with Harry, I asked him why he wanted to see me and his answer was: "How can I learn to make myself do what is right, and not always be in trouble?" He mentioned to me that he really wanted to do things that were right, but found himself often doing things that were wrong and because of this, many times the cost was pretty high. He said to me, "Just like now, I am here in jail, (prison language for being locked in solitary confinement) because I wanted a Coke and was willing to bend some rules so a friend would buy me one from the canteen.[5] The reason for this kind of rule in correctional facilities is that if an inmate gets into debt to another inmate, trouble can arise between the two and then spread to other 'friends'. The common rate of interest of borrowing from an inmate is, <u>100%</u>, and is often compounded on a weekly basis. These things can get out of hand very quickly. Often times the 'debt' is collected in flesh and blood.

This was the kind of trouble Harry now found himself in. Many times when an inmate gets into this kind of situation, they will write 'home' to have some family member send money to be put on the books of the inmate that they owe. But in the case of Harry (as is often the situation with many inmates), he did not have any outside 'support'.

As I knelt, stooped, and sat on the floor, visiting with Harry, (after about 15 minutes, a very kind officer brought a mop bucket and turned it upside down and suggested I might be more comfortable if I had something to sit on[6]), I asked Harry to read, out loud, (my reason for such a request was twofold: [1] for him to be sure to know it was in the Bible, and [2] that other inmates in the cells close by could also hear what we were talking about), Mathew 16:24 as I handed him a New Testament. As he read "......*let him deny himself......*" he looked up at me and said, "Does that mean I can't do things I enjoy?" Without answering his question, I told him to turn to the book of Hebrews in the New Testament, and after a little searching to find Hebrews, he said, "Where?" He seemed eager to get an answer to his question. I asked him to read chapter 11 and verses 24 & 25. *"By faith Moses, when he was come to years, refused to be called the son of Pharaoh's daughter; choosing rather to suffer affliction with the people of God, than to enjoy the pleasure of sin for a season;"*

---

[5] On prison yards this is called 'bartering'.

[6] (and he was really accurate with that comment.)

I asked him if he understood, why would Moses forgo the pleasure of the King's palace (being called the son of the Pharaoh's daughter)? He smiled as he answered my question, "I guess that Moses understood that there was something better than being the grandson of the ruler of Egypt." With that answer I let Harry know that he had indeed spoken truth, and that we could learn a very valuable lesson to help us (him) not to do the things that are wrong. After he read that, I asked him to consider that our Lord was more than ready to do things that were perhaps not what He would like to do, but willing to obey a higher authority.

Another section of scripture I asked him to read was; (Romans 7:15 – 17), *"For that which I do, I know not; For what I would, that do I not; but what I hate, that do I. If then I do that which I would not, I consent unto the law that it is good. Now then it is no more I that that do it, but sin that dwelleth in me. For I know that is, in my flesh dwelleth no good thing: for to will is present with me; but how to perform that which good I find not."* After we read it together, I pointed out that the context of the passage was dealing with keeping of the law of Moses, yet the truth that was conveyed by the apostle would be very applicable to his question, "Why do I always do things that get me in trouble?"

As we continued our study; remember that the inmate in the next cell could hear all our conversation, and I will never know if he paid any attention to what was being said; I then asked Harry to read the words of our Lord as recorded in Mathew 26:42. I left him to think on that, and told him I would be back the following Monday to continue our study.

> Into his late 50s, he had served more than 60% of his life in jails or prison. On one occasion, he spoke to me with these words, "When I am out, I want to be back in, and when I am in I want to be back out."

That conversation took place on Tuesday afternoon. I will never know how Harry was able to get a note to me so quickly, but in my mail the following Saturday was the following message, in its entirety:

> "I look forward toward our
> study next Tuesday.
>
> Harry"

When I returned to that facility the next Tuesday Harry was gone and I have never heard from, or about him since. I often wonder, "Did I present enough of God's Word to him, that he would learn not to do the things that always got him in trouble?"

My thoughts through the years since have been, "Did he go through his *'Life Without'* learning the self-discipline that we talked about that last visit I had with him?" I guess I will never know!

This kind of mind-set that Harry displayed, has caused many 'offenders' to return, 'over and over' again to jail and prison convictions. The term used in the language of correctional staff is, 'RECIDIVISM'. That is, 'to fall back' and the 'ism' at the end, perhaps with the idea of 'chronic or habitual'. On many occasions, I came in contact with inmates that had served multiple sentences. May we use "Albert" as a classic example. Albert had started his criminal activities as a teenager, taking things that were not his (for example his grandfather's car), then stealing from stores and moving on to armed robbery. Into his late 50s, he had served more than 60% of his life in jails or prison. On one occasion, he spoke to me with these words, "When I am out, I want to be back in, and when I am in I want to be back out." After I retired from traveling to the State Correctional facilities, the Owasso congregation continued to support the efforts to teach in the Tulsa County Jail, for the next 12 years. It was not unusual when I would go into one of the units to have an inmate come to me and ask if I remembered him from one of the facilities that it had been my pleasure to teach the Word of God. Sometimes the name (or face) might cause me to remember, but on many of those occasions I would have to ask where had I met them. Remember I came in contact with perhaps a thousand inmates a week. Have you ever heard the PHRASE, 'Life long criminal'? Let me assure you, indeed there are such people!

Chapter 8

Life Without…
An Understanding of Love

Remember in chapter 1, we read an inmate wrote, "Prison is a place where if you are married, you watch your marriage die." Indeed, this is true, but in many cases, there was not a Biblical understanding in the first place. This of course is not just inmates lack of understanding, for there are many in the free world who have never been incarcerated, find themselves in the same situation.

However, there is perhaps a greater percentage among those that find themselves (both male & female) in trouble with the law, because they have not been willing to submit to authority, whether it be physical or spiritual. I have had occasions to study with both men and women (though far more men than women) that were serving time in prisons and jails, who had never learned of the Lord's teaching concerning the sanctity of marriage.

It is not an unusual thing to hear vial, ungodly, ugly, or hateful comments

It is not an unusual thing to hear vial, ungodly, ugly, or hateful comments by inmates on prison yards; and often times it is not possible to try and speak in a manner to correct such language. However, it is important to make sure that those who utter such thoughts or words know that God's people do not use or approve such.

by inmates on prison yards; and often times it is not possible to try and speak in a manner to correct such language. However, it is important to make sure that those who utter such thoughts or words know that God's people do not use or approve such. One phrase that is often spoken by male inmates is, 'MY OLD LADY'. My response to this comment on many occasions was, "Why do you disrespect the one you say you LOVE?" More times than not I have had individuals respond with such comments as; "Oh, I meant to say, my wife", or "I should have given her more praise and thanks for putting up with me." It became almost a standing joke among those that were in my classes, to tell outsiders not to say 'My Old Lady' in front of me or they would be in line for a scolding.

But a much more serious problem was that of divorce and remarriage. This came up many times, especially when I was asked to perform a wedding, which happened many times in the more than 16 years of teaching in prisons. On many occasions in Bible classes, the subject of divorce would arise (remember I had the privilege of teaching in 10 different state facilities), and like any other subject, a Bible answer had to be presented.

On one occasion, almost a hundred volunteers (Bible teachers, both men & women from the Lord's church) from across the state of Oklahoma gathered to learn and teach each other the most effective means of teaching the lost in jails and prisons.

An ex-offender made in my hearing, at that gathering (I cannot quote his exact words), a statement that we should not be concerned about the question of an inmate's marriage, but just teach them the gospel. My first thought (which I made known to the elders of the sponsoring congregation where the meeting was held) was, "Can one become a Christian (obey the gospel) and not repent of sin?" How can I teach the gospel and not teach that one must repent of sin? And the sin of adultery must be repented of, as much as any other sin.

There were those that studied earnestly the scriptures concerning their relationships as marriages that were not what the Lord ordained. One such young man, (we shall know him as "Ken") that was with one of our classes in the first or second year of our labors in jail/prison evangelism, wrote me a later over five or six years after he had completed his sentence. He had moved to a state on the east coast, finished his secular college education and looked forward to enrolling in Southern Christian University to work for his master's degree in Christian counseling, then onto the East Tennessee School of Preaching. The following is a part of the letter he sent to me:

> "I guess I was a little shocked about some of the worldly attitudes that I ran into concerning my decision to get out of an unscriptural marriage." (The woman he had married to had been married twice before, and in his letter he added,) "While I was getting help, my wife, (an active drug addict) left me for another man. Upon completing my sentence, I started considering a possible reconciliation with her, but after studying the scriptures, and taking her two previous unscriptural divorces into consideration, I realized it was not God's will that I should stay in the marriage. ......"

Through many years Ken has been consistent to keep in contact with me by mail. He has shared with me news about gaining custody of his two daughters, and their growth in the faith of the living God which he had learned. He has told me of their baptisms, their growth in the Lord, and their growing into young ladies that are dating young Christian men that are faithful workers in the kingdom of God. In one of his last letters, he wrote:

> "...... It is wonderful to hear from you. Especially of the good news if all the baptisms. That is great! ...... When I think back to the fellowship we had at RTTB, (a minimum facility at Lexington. *rdh*) and since then, it makes me feel proud to call you my

> brother and friend. ...... I have some
> good news myself: First of all, as a
> result of a Bible study, I was able to
> baptize a soul into Christ. This is the
> first successful direct study that I
> have been able to complete. I was
> also the one to do the actual bap-
> tism."

Later in that same letter he mentioned that he was sad that he had never been able to convince his mother that she needed to obey the Lord in baptism.

Let me make it clear at this point, I did not encourage inmates getting married while serving time, though I did do two weddings in such circumstance. The following is the reason I did conduct these weddings. The first was a man (let's use the name, "Walter".) Walter was serving three (3), life sentences. In the language of the inmates, 'running wild'. In the early years of his confinement, his mother brought a young lady with her to visit Walter. In a very ungodly, as well as illegal action, Walter and the young girl, somehow hid in a broom closet, and committed fornication. It was more than 25 years later that Walter learned he had fathered a daughter. The girl that had birthed Walter's child had never married. It was another eight or so years that Walter sat in one of our classes (in a different facility) and the study was in I Corinthians 5. After the class, Walter asked if I would come to his cell the next day and study more on the subject of marriage? I answered in the affirmative, and it was in that study of about 90 minutes he asked if I would be willing to perform a wedding for them. Some two weeks later, with the chaplain, deputy warden, and two correctional officers as witness, the wedding took place in the chaplain's office. A request for the daughter to be allowed to attend was denied.

The second wedding I conducted came about as a result of another study, at a different facility I had conducted. "Vernon" asked in the class the question, "If I had children (plural) with a woman, but had never married, would I be right with God?" I answered by suggesting we get together in a private conversation, and he was willing to do so. On my next visit to that facility (a week later), Vernon was waiting almost at the gate when I entered the yard. We went to his cell (he had asked his 'cellie' to absent himself) and he told me his story.

Let me insert here an event that demonstrates his willingness to take on any challenge, knowing he was without doubt, the 'underdog'. Vernon was not a large individual, but one that was not intimidated by someone bigger than himself. He was well aware that any physical confrontation (fight) with another inmate would mean some kind of, 'write-up'. Which could mean perhaps a period of time in solitary confinement; loss of 'good time' (days erased from sentence); or even worse, more time added to one's conviction. Knowing these things, yet he had a problem with a much larger inmate. His answer to this dilemma was to meet this other inmate in the gym, during a period of regular physical exercise, with supervision of guards, and engage in a 'boxing match'. This would not be a 'fight' which could result in some kind of 'write-up', but satisfy the much larger inmate, to settle the score with Vernon.

He began by telling me how he had met the mother of his children. At some sort of gathering (certainly not a Christian atmosphere) a young lady, (may we use the name "Mary") was being tormented because of her weight. There were three boys who were verbally abusing Mary, and Vernon 'rode' to her rescue, not even knowing her. Though being outnumbered, Vernon soon had the three in full retreat and Mary seeing her 'knight' as one she wanted to know better. From that moment, the two began a relationship that led to an ungodly one that eventually brought two children into the world. Vernon & Mary lived together for almost three years before he was arrested.

Vernon had completed about half of his 10-year sentence when the question about his having children with Mary came up. As we studied such passages as I Corinthians 6:9 - 10 and Ephesians 5:3, dealing with fornication, being listed among other actions that would keep one out of the Lord's kingdom, he asked me if I would be willing to marry he and Mary. I answered in the affirmative, and as in the case with Walter and his wife the wedding took place with only the Unit Manager, two Correctional officers, Mary, and Vernon present. However, the warden did allow the couple to have a wedding cake to be shared with a few of Vernon's friends (inmates) in the visiting room after the ceremony was completed.

These were the only two weddings I had a part, in the 26+ years dealing with jail/prison evangelism. In fact, I turned down many requests to perform weddings, encouraging the incarcerated (both male & female), to postpone such plans until their sentences were completed. However, I did on many occasions teach lessons about breaking up unscriptural marriages.

Turning the coin over from teaching about getting out of unscriptural marriages, it was a joy teaching about the blessings of God ordained marriage. It was a great time that I learned of two ex-felons that returned to their wives (much like the story we find in the book of Hosea), to restore that which they had committed to do (be husband & wife) many years before they found themselves in prison. One of those inmates has passed from this life (his wife is also deceased), but the other lives in a very loving relationship at this present time. Not only is the joy of a Christian family shared by this brother and his wife, but even a greater blessing knowing that their Father in Heaven is pleased.

Chapter 9

Life Without...
A Feeling of Guilt

In the Gospel of Luke chapter 18 and verses 11 – 12, we have the thought of a man rejoicing in the thinking that he was not as guilty of sin as other men. *"The Pharisee stood and prayed, thus to himself, God, I thank thee, that I am not as other men are, extortioners, unjust, adulterers, or even as this publican. I fast twice in the week, I give tithes of all that I posses."*

Let me introduce you to three inmates, two females and one male. The first lady we will meet came as a result of being in a class that it was my joy to have had the opportunity to speak to the group of ladies that came to a Bible Class in the chapel of David L. Moss Correctional Center (Tulsa County Jail). Keep in mind that male volunteers are not allowed to go into the female pods. The opportunity to have this class only lasted about six weeks (the new Tulsa County Jail was first

In the Gospel of Luke chapter 18 and verses 11 – 12, we have the thought of a man rejoicing in the thinking that he was not as guilty of sin as other men. *"The Pharisee stood and prayed, thus to himself, God, I thank thee, that I am not as other men are, unjust, adulterers, or even as this publican. I fast twice in the week, I give tithes of all that I posses."*

run by a private company known as 'CCA' (Correction Company of America)), and when the jail was returned to Tulsa County Sheriff's control, my Wednesday evening class was not allowed to continue.[7]

On the second Wednesday night of our Bible Class, "Lucy" informed me that she was classified as a 'trustee', and was allowed to work in a county office in Owasso, being transported by a Tulsa police car as far as the city limits of Owasso, where she would be transferred to the Owasso police car, to be taken to her assigned work place. In the evening the reverse of the morning was carried out. In our Bible study the subject came up of meeting with the Lord's body to worship. In her trial, her conviction was passed down and she was given I believe, a one year sentence, and after she went through A&R[8] she was returned to the facility that is now known as Turley Correctional Facility. That facility was the old Turley Children's Home (a work of the Lord's church for many years) which was sold to the state of Oklahoma. The facility was a 'Work Release' type center that allowed inmates with 'clean' records to receive a pass. Some for 6 hours and some for as much as 12 hours. This was allowed as long as the inmate was checked out by a badged volunteer, (and was returned to the facility *before* the appointed time ended!) And as I had a badge (from several different facilities), Lucy was often allowed to come to the Owasso congregation for worship service on Sunday mornings. After she completed her sentence, she returned to her home community, and the last I heard she was still faithfully attending services in a congregation near her home, in the Oklahoma City area.

One Sunday morning as we were coming to Bible study and worship services, she began telling me (and another member of the congregation; for I never was alone with a female inmate), about her conviction. She had been charged with 'embezzlement'. As she talked very openly in the van with myself as well as the other sister, her comments were somewhat like the Pharisee, saying "I didn't do any more than others in my office." So, we had a good Bible study just between the three of us for the 20 minutes of our travel from Turley to Owasso.

---

[7]A side note; I informed the chaplain that I would not go into the chapel without a Uniformed Female officer in the room!

[8]Assignment & Reassignment

The second female inmate, we will know her as, "Beverly". I met Beverly through having a study with another female inmate that we have met in an earlier chapter. Her charge was 'failing' to protect a minor! The man she was living with had abused her 2-year-old child, which resulted in the death of the child. Beverly had been incarcerated some 32 months before I met her. Her lawyers and her 'fall partner's' (this is a familiar term used by inmates, dealing with those charged in the case), would constantly object to whatever the other would present, thus causing the trial to be 'continued' until that point was cleared up, thus her time in the county jail had almost reached the three-year mark.

Beverly never, in my studies with her, expressed any kind of thought that she was as the Pharisee in Luke 18, but there was a constant denial on her part that she had any part of the child's death. When the trial was finally set, and the jury heard the case, Beverly was given a sentence of 15 years, with the credit of 'time served' (the 32 months + good time). This was in 1996 and due to overcrowding in state facilities Oklahoma Corrections sent many female inmates to private correctional facilities in Texas. Beverly was among those, and I lost track of her. As a result, I do not know what our studies with her accomplished.

The third inmate I want to introduce you, is an older man, perhaps over 60 years old. "Carl" (not his real name), was in a county jail (not Tulsa) and had been arrested for child molestation. I was contacted by members of the congregation he attended, and drove to the city where he was in jail to visit with him. As I introduced myself, and told him who had made contact with me about his arrest, the first thing he said to me was; "Those who accused me are lying, I don't have any idea why they are saying those things about me. They must really be mad at me about something, and I don't know what it is." After a very short trial, Carl was sentenced and, as far as I know, never admitted his guilt to man or God. The passage of scripture I left with him that visit was I John 1:7 – 10, with emphasis on verses 9 & 10, *"**IF** we confess our sins, He is faithful and just to forgive us our sins, and to cleanse us from all unrighteousness. If we say that we have not sinned, we make Him a liar, and His word is **NOT** in us."* It is my prayer that he will do (or has done) as the apostle John wrote.

Chapter 10

Life Without...
A Number

Every inmate, state or federal, is given a number. That number is his 'identity' within the system. Just as each of us have our own set of fingerprints, unique from all other people, so also the inmate with his number. An individual that finishes his sentence, however long that might be, will always have that number. Should he ever be arrested again that number will again be assigned to him.

This was brought to the attention of a group of young people as an ex-offender, that I had the

> Out of prison? Yes, but for as long as he lived there would always be that number after his name on state records.

joy of baptizing into Christ while he was incarcerated, stood before the gathering at a youth rally in an eastern Oklahoma town. There were some sixty to seventy in attendance as the young man told of the years of drug abuse that had led to his incarceration. As he spoke, he rolled up the sleeve of his shirt to reveal a number of tattoos. He continued his talk as he pointed to these and said that even as he would always have the tattoos on his arms, so would he always have a number. Out of prison? Yes, but for as long as he lived there would always be that number after his name on state records.

David wrote in Psalms 51:2-3, *"Wash me thoroughly from my iniquity, and cleanse me from my sin. For I acknowledge my transgressions: and my sin is ever before me."* All ex-felons will have this sword of Damocles hanging above them but many who have indeed learned a hard-earned lesson never let it bother them. Although they know, just as the psalmist knew about his sin, their past, many of them go on to lead a very productive life. Both in the physical realm as well as the spiritual, mankind has to face the consequences of his actions. In the physical, one might have to pay the fine, whatever that might be, and in the spiritual realm mankind must also pay for his sins *"For we must all appear before the judgment seat of Christ; that every one may receive the things done in his body, according to all that he hath done, whether it be good or bad."* (II Corinthians 5:10) The great difference is that there has been a redeemer who is able and willing to expunge all sin if we will obey His will.

What are the results of always having a number? I borrow a thought from the book of Romans (taken out of context of course) 3:1 & 2; what advantage then has the man that does not have a D.O.C. number behind his name? Or, to look on the other side of the coin, we might ask, "What consequence does the one that has a number have to face?" Just as the apostle answered the spiritual question, so we can have the same answer in this physical scenario, "Much in every way." Different crimes of course are treated in different ways, for example one convicted of theft will face a lifetime of having to answer to every potential employer, "Can you be trusted?" For one who was convicted of writing checks that had insufficient funds it will take years to be able to purchase something with a check, without having to verify the validity and value of that piece of paper.

> Different crimes of course are treated in different ways, for example one convicted of theft will face a lifetime of having to answer to every potential employer, "Can you be trusted?"

An 'ex-felon' will always have to give an answer to a prospective employer, about the nature of his or her conviction. And in many instances, it will result in a rejection of the individual getting the job. And to withhold the truth about the fact, at some time when it comes to light, (and it will), much like the last statement made in Matthew 12:45, (again taken of course out of context) *"...... the last state of that man is worse than the first......"*

Our present world is filled with 'numbers': bank account numbers; car tag numbers; social security number; telephone numbers; street address numbers, and on and on. But the convicted felon; perhaps only a short time in prison with only a minor crime, still will as we noted early in this chapter, have a number for life.

As strange as it might seem, as we have already been made aware, every inmate has a number. That D.O.C. (Department of Corrections) number is more likely be used when the staff addresses the inmate than his (or her) name. It is as if the individual is no longer a person, just an object to answer to authority. I vividly recall one occasion when I had made a request to take a young man that desired to be baptized into Christ, from his cell to the chapel where there was a facility to accomplish the baptism, that when I talked with the chaplain to make arrangement to take him to the chapel to accomplish his desires, the chaplain did not write the inmates name on the order for him be allowed to cross the yard, but his 6 digit DOC#.

There is however one situation in which a felon would desire a <u>number</u> behind his name! It is called in the language of inmates; having <u>numbers</u> behind their conviction, rather than <u>letters</u>. For example: Joe Convict, serving 20 years is much more desired than: Joe Convict, serving LIFE. Those that had a number of days or years, had at least something to hope for, while those with letters had nothing to look forward to. Let me give you a couple of examples of men that I had the joy of seeing both obey the Gospel. The first we shall call "Charles". The second will be to us, "Wes". Charles was convicted and sentenced to, 'undetermined' time. Wes was convicted and given LIFE! Both men appealed (their sentence, not their convictions) and after almost 20 years, both won their cases; Charles was given a set amount of years, and was released just a few months after the appeal was granted.[9] Three years after Wes was given a number of years, he served the number of years of his sentence, and the last I heard of him he was living in Oklahoma City.

---

[9]A few months after his release he visited our worship services here in Owasso.

Chapter 11

Life Without...
Getting Any Mail

It was heart breaking to see inmates line up when the mail list was posted and to see the face of those that did not find their names on it. As I would watch some of them that I knew did not receive much mail, not even go check the list. On one occasion I asked one such individual why he didn't check to see if he had received mail? His answer was, "What's the use? No one ever writes to me." This is another point that Wayne had written to me about that rings loud in my memory. Remember his second point that we read about in Chapter 1? He said that one in prison writes fewer and fewer letters, and finally just quits writing altogether because there just wasn't anything he could think about to write.

There could be several reasons a prisoner might not get mail nor send any. One is that family has forsaken the individual that is imprisoned. Why have some families followed this approach? For many it is be-

> On one occasion an inmate called me into his cell to show me a stack of letters he had sent to some members of his family that had been returned to him.

cause the prisoner has been habitual in his actions, being placed back in prison repeatedly for the same kind of offence. On one occasion an inmate called me into his cell to show me a stack of letters he had sent to some members of his family that had been returned to him. We need to take note here that anytime a letter is sent out from an inmate, on the back of the envelope is stamped a notice that the material comes from an incarcerated individual. I had one fellow about 65 to 70 years old that told me that he was doing his fourth sentence and that he had not heard from any of his brothers or sisters in over 20 years. In a lengthy conversation with him, he told me, "I am just a thief, and I really am rightfully here. I am not like so many others that say they are innocent and should not be here. But, I wish that my family would at least acknowledge that I exist."

An inmate (we shall call him "Richard") that had obeyed the gospel and was very regular in Bible study and worship service that is held at that facility by the Lord's church, was thrilled when the congregation of the church here in Owasso, placed his name on their mailing list to send the weekly bulletin from the congregation to him every two weeks. Each time that the bulletin was to arrive he would stand in line, sometimes 30 minutes to get 'his mail'. He would invite me to his cell and proudly show me what he had received, and proceed to tell me all the things that were written in it. Of course, I already knew what was there, for many times I had written part of it. But just the fact that his name was on the mail list he would say, as Clint Eastwood might say, "Made my day."

Three or four years after Richard started receiving his weekly 'mail' from the congregation I was surprised as he called me into his cell to show me a newspaper clipping he had received in that day's mail from his son. The clipping was about his grandchild that had won a bicycle from some contest that the police from his hometown had sponsored. The thrill Richard got from getting that piece of mail was tempered by the only note that came with it, his son asking the inmate if he could borrow money from him.

Many times inmates not receiving mail took the absence of mail as an indication something was very wrong at home.

It was not always a feeling of something wrong at home when there was not mail, sometime it was just a feeling that the world had forgotten them, or that 'inmates' were not worth remembering.

Of course, this was not always true but it was not unusual for this to be the case. This might range from a family member being very ill (or even a death having taken place) to perhaps a relationship breaking up. I do not have the exact data, but I do know that a great number of marriages are dissolved while the husband or wife is incarcerated, and in some cases when both are in prison. This can be as a result of the actions of the mates that brought about the confinement, or as in many cases just the absence of the mate.

It was not always a feeling of something wrong at home when there was not mail, sometime it was just a feeling that the world had forgotten them, or that 'inmates' were not worth remembering. I received the following letter (just a portion of the letter) from a young man that was incarcerated in an east coast state. (We have met this inmate in chapter 4.):

"Dear bro. Ralph, Greeting in the name of Christ, our Saviour and King! WOW! Where do I start?? Words fail to express the overwhelming joy I now have. Your letter today was received with tears of joy. I could not convey in any human language the gratitude that I have for your sincere kindness. Thank you! Thank you! Thank you! ...... In August of last year, (2002 *rdh*) I began publishing a monthly newsletter entitled, 'PRISON EPISTLE from _____'. I sent it to over 300 Churches of Christ, mostly in North Carolina, but also in Tennessee, Indiana, Oklahoma, and Ohio. I also began writing to many preachers in the brotherhood, but to my dismay, I received hardly no response. You could imagine my disappointment. I learned a valuable lesson. The church

that exists today is not exactly like
the first century A.D. church of
Christ. ...... Anyway, I actually received a tract that was personally
sent by brother McCord, I am still at
a loss at how he received my address.
That is what initiated the letter that
I wrote him. I was going to write him
last year, but after being ignored by
so many others, I decided not to write
him. When I received such a prompt
response, I was very happy and surprised. I talk on the phone periodi-
cally to a local gospel preacher and
told him that receiving a letter from
Hugo McCord was like getting a letter
from the President of the United
States, except better! We got a good
laugh out of that!"

Because of Calvary, I am your
brother in Christ,

C____ M ____

Chapter 12

Life Without…
An Expectation of Something Better

In the apostle Paul's great lesson in I Corinthians 15 concerning the hope that comes through the Gospel of Christ a statement is recorded in verse 19. *"If in this life only we have hope in Christ, we are of all men most miserable;"* that often came to mind as I spoke with inmates. Remember from chapter one that a young man had written an essay to me and had made the point (number 3) "Prison is a place where hopes spring eternal. Where each parole appearance means a chance to get out even if the odds are hopelessly against you."

One of the first individuals I met after starting our work in prison/ jail mission efforts under the Owasso eldership oversight, was a man that we shall call "Troy". We have met this man in the preface of this book. Troy received

> I had lost contact with him, not knowing where he had been sent, so I was very surprised as a voice called out, "Hi, Ralph!"

a life sentence for taking two lives in a rage during a domestic argument. Troy had spent over a year in the county jail while the court was conducting his trial. The reason for such a long delay seemed to be that the district attorney desired a 'death' sentence, but Troy wanted to plead guilty and even the girl's mother had asked that he not be given the death penalty. Her reasoning was based on the thought that the daughter had been part to blame for the fight that preceded her death. Several years later I came in contact with Troy at one of the facilities I visited each week. I had lost contact with him, not knowing where he had been sent, so I was very surprised as a voice called out, "Hi, Ralph!" When I turned toward the voice, there stood Troy. To say the least, that after almost 15 years, not only would I run into him again but for him to call me by name!

Perhaps I should not have been as surprised as I was, for he had asked me to conduct his mother's funeral the first year after he was sent to prison, and remembering the preface of this book he was the inmate that had first requested for me to come visit with him. (I might add that two other inmates requested that I might take part in memorial services for family members, in addition to Troy's mother.)

Our conversation, after a very warm and happy greeting, turned to asking him how he was doing and perhaps what was the outlook for his future. His answer was something like, "I really have no hope of ever being paroled, I probably will die in prison." The next question I asked him was, had he continued his study of God's Word that had begun in the county jail? Unfortunately, his answer was in the negative. And even more unfortunate, that was the last time I visited on that yard.

In chapter 1, you read the comments of an inmate that wrote about "PRISON IS A PLACE". In his third (3rd) comment he talked about "hope springs eternal" even when the odds seem to be against you. After I retired from full time going into state facilities, I received the following note (a small part) from a student I had for several years.

> "......by God's grace I have made parole through the 'jacket review & Personal Appearance with the board, (word of explanation: To those not familiar with 'prison terms', "jacket review" is the written report of every action and conduct of the inmate in all the time he was incarcerated. [write ups; any time spent in "D.U."; obedience of commands; etc.]) and signed my (Certificate of Parole) to

the governor. As soon as she signs it and my home offer is verified with my brother and sister-in-law in Colorado, I can go home to be with my loved ones and friends after 31 years."

Not all those who find themselves in prison have the 'REWARD' of even a parole. The next inmate we will meet, has a far different ending. We will just identify him as "John". I heard of this man in the newspaper and on TV. John had killed his wife and daughters, then turned himself into the police. I went the next day to the county jail where he was incarcerated and asked the jailer if he would see me.

> He immediately began to sob and tell me what a terrible thing he had done, never making any excuse, just saying he would have to go before the judge of all men, not the judge of men's law. His trial was a very speedy one and he was given the death penalty.

In a few minutes, he was brought to the visiting area where I was assigned, and shackled to the wall in front of me. When I told him who I was, his first words were that he knew me for he was a member of a congregation where I had spoken about our jail/prison mission effort. He immediately began to sob and tell me what a terrible thing he had done, never making any excuse, just saying he would have to go before the judge of all men, not the judge of men's law. His trial was a very speedy one and he was given the death penalty.

John requested immediate transport to prison, and like all convicted felons, was sent to Lexington (the facility is known as LARC, which stands for: Lexington Assessment Relocation Center.) From LARC he was sent to McAlester ('Big Mac') and was placed on death row. Unlike so many that we hear about that make appeal after appeal, and may spend upward to 15 or 20 years on death row before being executed, John refused to make any appeal. He spent less than a year on death row, before he was put to death. My letter to him was never answered, but I will always remember my first and last visit with him, in which he stated, "I must face the God of heaven!"

Let me introduce you to "Bill", a member of the Lord's church in the state of Texas. I have no idea of the reason he was in prison, nor the length of his sentence. In my correspondence with him there was never a mention of his crime or conviction, only that he was in his early 70s, and that he, in the first letter I received from him, made mention that without a successful appeal of his conviction he would die in prison.[10] I have not had any contact with Bill in the intervening 25 or so years. And after so many years (remember, Moses wrote in Psalm 90:10; *The days of our years are threescore years and ten; and if by reason of strength they be fourscore years, yet is their strength labour and sorrow; for it is soon cut off, and we fly away.*"), I can only surmise, that one way or another (in prison or released), he has passed from this life to await the judgment of the Lord as we note the message written in Hebrews 9:27 (*And as it is appointed unto men once to die, but after this the judgment.*) If Bill was more than 70 when I last had contact with him, he would be at least 96 or more years old at this present time.

Bill and John were not the only inmates that I met in the 30+ years of going into jails and prisons that died while incarcerated. Even those that had relatively short sentences sometimes failed to find something better. Many who did not have a *'Life Without'* sentence, still did not have an exemption from death.

The expectations of something better often times failed to materialize. Let me introduce you to "Cliff", a young man that was well liked by many of the inmates and respected by the staff. He was never in a class with me, and as far as I know was not ever involved in anything of a spiritual nature. However, he was always very respectful of my presence, and I never heard him use any vulgar, rude, or unkind language; nor did I ever know him to belittle or discourage those that practiced anything spiritual.

---

[10]Bill had been in contact with Buster Dobbs, editor of *Firm Foundation*, who had sent Bill a copy of Jerry Frazier's book, *Fundamental Facts, Simply Explained* from which he got the Owasso church's address.

Cliff completed his short time in prison, (I heard that he served less than a 5-year sentence.) and returned to his home town. The next day the yard where he had done his time was alive with the news that Cliff had been killed in an auto accident, the night he got home. Several of his friends on the yard came to me with this news. AN EXPECTATION of something better? I used this illustration many times with those I had opportunity to teach on that yard.

I do not have the statistics at hand, but the reality is evident that the greatest majority of inmates complete their sentences and return their lives to live again in their normal manner as before they were incarcerated. Even many of those that were given the sentence, '*Life Without*'. Of course, the percentage of those is much lower than those who did not have such a sentence. There are those however that had much less severe sentence, that never get out 'alive'.[11]

Let me introduce you to two of these cases that it was my lot to be aware, though I did not know one of these men personally. "Will" was a cellmate of a man that became a very dedicated disciple of our Lord (we have met this man in an earlier chapter.) Will was in his 'mid-seventies' and was serving a sentence of less than a dozen years. "Charles", I would guess, was less than 30 years of age. I have no idea of his charge, nor sentence.

It was not unusual for those in a 'minimum' facility not to get up for the early breakfast call (6:30), as many of these inmates were transported to work locations away from the facility. If the inmate was absent for the 'count' at breakfast, the officer in charge of that unit would go to the cell of the inmate to see if indeed was present. In the case of Will, he was still in his bunk and the officer thought him to be asleep. At the 11:00 A.M. count the officer looked in and saw Will in the same position. Going into the cell, the officer found that Will had apparently died in the night.

In Charles' case, there had been some kind of dispute with another inmate (or group), that had been going on for some period of time. I never knew (nor did I want to know), about the details. I just was told as I went to check in to visit on the yard that morning, "the yard was closed", the cause -- there had been a murder on the yard the night before. Charles had been beaten with a brick while he was sleeping.

---

[11]I need to make known here that a 'life' sentence in the Law, is considered as 45 years.

One other death of an inmate, with whom that I had opportunity to correspond.[12] I have written about him in an earlier chapter of this writing. His case was known around the world, and without doubt was hideous. I had several people ask me if I thought he could be forgiven of his crime. I gave the following answer: "Was the apostle Paul forgiven for his persecuting the church as revealed in Acts chapters 9 and 22?" This young man was killed by another inmate in a facility of a state in the northeast.

Beside physical death taking place to inmates, there are those that, 'like many older people', face such illnesses as, Alzheimer's disease, or other types of brain damage, some caused by use of drugs. Let me introduce you to two men with such illness. The first was an older gentleman in his late 60s, serving his sentence as a 'sex offender' in a minimum facility. There were no fences or steel bars surrounding the facility, just an open field about three or four hundred yards before a very large lake. I heard the radio call to a nearby yard officer, a command from the Unit's manager's office, to "go get inmate (#112233?) Mr. "Smith", he is headed toward the lake." Mr. Smith answered the officer's question of, "Where are you going?" with the simple statement, "To the store to a get a loaf of bread for my wife." The officer walked him back to the compound with words something like, "That's all right, Smitty, the kitchen staff has already been to the store to get what they need."

The second man we will meet is an individual (may we identify him as, "Cotton") that had been released some twenty years before this event. In fact, he and his mother[13] have attended a congregation of the Lord's church in a community near Oklahoma City, for over 10 years. It was 9 or 10 years after I had stopped going into state facilities I received a very strange phone call from Cotton. He wanted me to help him by calling the Oklahoma City police to get them to, "Stop their helicopters spying on him every night, and keeping him awake." He had tried to get the elders of the congregation to help him, but they ignored his request. This of course was all in the imagination of a 'brain' that had been saturated with drugs and booze, for no telling how many years.

---

[12] I never met this young man, knowing him only through the brother that baptized him and the letters between us.

[13] He obeyed the Gospel while in prison, and she became a Christian , as a result of his teaching her what he had learned in prison.

Chapter 13

Life Without…
Encouragement from Other Inmates

In the New Testament the Hebrew letter contains the admonishment to *"exhort one another: and so much the more, as you see the day approaching."* (10:25b) Whoever the writer was, the Holy Spirit inspired him to pass on that Christians need to be encouraged. Why? Satan will use every means possible to steal away one's allegiance from the Father in heaven.

Not only is there a need of fellowship of fellow prisoners in jails and prisoners, but the need of fellowship of the Christians from the home congregation of inmates. Oh, yes! There are Christ -ians that are overtaken by sin, and find themselves in our prison system. In the beginning of the Owasso's congregation to be involved in jail/prison evangelism, the idea of just converting souls to truth, but also restoring the lost Christian. (James 5:19-20 teaches us: *"Brethren, If any of you do err from the truth, and one covert him; let him know that he which converteth the sinner from the error of his way, shall save a soul from death, and shall hide a multitude of sins."*)

With this in mind, the following letter had a great deal of meaning.

> "My name is Jim _____ . I am
> #???????. I am 46 years old with a
> wife, an adopted son age 24, a step
> daughter age 21, and a step son age
> 14.
>
> Either this week or next, I will be
> transported to Lexington for A&R. I

am paying two years to the state for drunk driving.

The purpose of this letter is to ask you to please watch for me. I am aware of the services you have at Lexington, and want very much to be included. I was raised in the church of Christ, and in 1960 – 61 attended Oklahoma Christian College where I was blessed to study at the feet of brother Hugo McCord.

I still study everything I can about the Bible and our redeeming Christ. I have completed the entire Liberty Home Bible Course. Some of it was tough because I had to put down some answers they wanted that I know were wrong. Like Faith only, music in church (instrumental), and once saved always saved, Thank the Lord and my parents I was raised to know truth.

At my home congregation is where I first saw a letter from you about the work you do for prisoners. I was highly impressed although at that time I had no intention of becoming a prisoner myself. I now see the importance of a total commitment to God. He expects no less.

......, but I would be so thankful if you would be watching for me. I look forward to meeting you.

I am one that has not had a jail-house conversion, but I have come to

a strong rededication of my life to
God. Perhaps I can be of some use to
you while I am at Lexington.

Thank God for the blessing He
gives us by forgiving our sins.

May God be with you in your work
at Owasso.

In chapter 4 we read about a young man (never named, but
from another state) dealing with the news of his mother's death.
Listen now to three of his letters, (all dealing in some way with
lack of encouragement from fellow inmates, as well from the free
world.)

"COPING WITH CAPTIVITY" ......

"The subject of captivity is one
that abounds in the pages of Holy
Writ. From the captivity of the
patriarch Joseph, to the exile of the
beloved apostle John to the Isle of
Patmos, God's word is full of such
examples. There are many aspects of
captivity that are revealed in God's
word in regard to coping with not
losing hope in what would seem to be
the most dismal situation. For this
reason, this study will examine the
apostle Paul and how he was able to
cope with his captivity, and how, in
light of what the scriptures teach, we
too can cope with any form of
captivity."

In examining the life work of the
apostle Paul, one can only be
encouraged by his selfless deeds and

his fervent desire to serve Jesus with his whole being. What is revealed in the life of this faithful servant of God is the depth and breadth of power wielded by our sovereign Jehovah. Paul's commitment to deny self that Christ might be exalted in everything he did is so beautifully portrayed in his inspired epistles that make up half of the New Testament cannon. How did Paul deal with his captivity? What things were on his mind as he was held against his will? As we examine these characteristics of Paul, let us keep before us these solemn words he penned by inspiration of the Holy Spirit; *"Be ye followers of me, even as I am of Christ"* (I Corinthians 11:1)

The desire to please God led Paul all over the world proclaiming the gospel of Jesus Christ, fulfilling the commission given by his Master (Matt. 28:18 – 20; Mk. 16:15-16) He went from city to city, being mocked, beaten, chased away; all out of desire to serve God. Paul's commitment was displayed so clearly when, after he had been stoned in Lystra and left to die; he went on to Derbe, and then he went back through Lystra and all of the other places to encourage the new converts (Acts 14:21 – 22) What courage displayed by this faithful servant of God.

After Paul has been arrested in Jerusalem and carried to Caesarea, he was held captive for two years for no wrongdoing. During this time, he was frequently asked to speak to Felix and his wife Drusilla, as well as Festus. It was at the request of King Agrippa and Bernice that Paul gave one of his most compelling speeches where we can easily ascertain what he was most concerned with.

Recorded in Acts 26, Paul began to declare his life to King Agrippa and to all of the principal men of the city. I can only imagine the comfort and confidence Paul had in knowing that Jesus had prophesied about such events. *"And ye shall be brought before Governors and kings for my sake, foe a testimony against them and the Gentiles. But when they delver you up, take no thought how or what ye shall speak: for it shall be given you in that same hour what ye shall speak."* (Matt. 10:18 – 19)

As one reads through the account of Paul's defense before King Agrippa, one can only wonder with amazement at his obvious selflessness. Paul's entire defense was void of any plea for his release. In fact, he only mentions his imprisonment at the end of his speech. What then, was Paul's concern? *"Then Agrippa said unto Paul, Almost thou persuadest me to be a Christian. And Paul said, I would to*

God, that not only thou, but also all that hear me this day, were both almost and altogether such as I am, except for these bonds" (Acts 26:28 – 29) O' how misplaced our priorities are!

Paul's desire to be heavenly-minded is seen all throughout his "Prison epistles". *"If ye then be risen with Christ, seek those things which are above, where Christ sitteth on the right hand of God. Set your affection on things above, not on things on the earth"* (Col. 3:1 – 20) Paul coped with his captivity by remaining content. His contentment and joy is revealed when he penned these words to the church at Philippi; *"Rejoice in the Lord always: and again I say, Rejoice"* (Phil. 4:4)

He then goes on to talk about being content in every situation, even in prison. But how, we may ask, can anyone be content while being held captive? Verse eight supplies the answer: *"Finally, breather, whatsoever things are true, whatsoever things are honest, whatsoever things are just, whatsoever things are pure, whatsoever things are of good report: if there be any praise, think on these things."* Only by conforming our thoughts to that of our heavenly Father can we find joy and hope in the most adverse conditions.

Leading up to Paul's final moments on this earth, he never

failed to lose sight of his purpose, which was proclaiming Jesus as the Christ. Paul was mature, spiritual and committed. He never failed to express his dependence of God's infallible word (II Tim.2:9; 3:16-17), nor did he fail to express his dependency on Christ. (Phil. 3:7 – 8)

When his sojourn on this earth was winding down, he embraced his final demise, *"For I am now ready to be offered, and the time of my departure is at hand. I have fought the good fight, I have finished my course, I have kept the faith: Henceforth there is laid up for me a crown of righteousness, which the Lord, the righteous judge, shall give me at that day: and not to me only, but unto all them also that love His appearance"* (II Tim. 4:6 – 8) The hope and faith that Paul manifested in what would be to us the most difficult situation, is all that we need to cope with the most dire circumstances.

Many today are being held captive to sin. In their present state, they are separated from God and await eternal condemnation. This type of captivity, however, can be coped with just as Paul coped with his material captivity. Yet, we must heed the words of the apostle Paul; *"I beseech you therefore brethren, by the mercies of God, that you present your bodies a living sacrifice, holy, acceptable unto God, which is your reasonable service.*" (Romans 12:1) It is denying self, keeping your thoughts on God, and serving your fellow man that will break the bonds of captivity and bring a liberty you never imagined.

Examining the captivity of Paul and his approach to coping with his imprisonment has been a comfort to me. I can relate and know firsthand how Paul succeeded in overcoming the emotional overload of captivity. For even as I pen these words, I do so from behind prison walls. It is through the hope and promises of Jesus Christ that I, like Paul, am able to rejoice, even when being held captive. It is my hope and prayer that no matter what adversity you may face, that you never lose sight of *"the end of your faith, even the salvation of your souls"* (I Pet.1:9) *"Now unto Him that is able to keep you from falling, and to present you faultless before the presence of His glory with exceeding joy, to the only wise God our savior, be glory and majesty, dominion and power, both now and ever"* (Jude 24 – 25)

The following is 'some of a letter' I received from the young man that wrote the essays above.

"Dear brother,
Greetings in the name of Christ,

our saviour and King! WOW! Where do I start??? Words fail to express the over whelming joy I now have. Your letter today (the date of the letter was 4-2-2003. *rdh*) was received with tears of joy. I could never convey in any human language the gratitude that I have for your sincere kindness. Thank You! Thank You! Thank You!

The last eight months have been pretty crazy for me. I am located at a Federal Correctional Complex near _____. Within this complex, there is a medium security, low security, minimum security, and a Federal Medical Center. I spent almost five years at the Low security prison and was recently transferred to the minimum-security prison complex; this move took place on Dec. 19th, 2002. This place is very laid back. There is no fence and very little supervision. I have a great deal of time to study God's perfect word, and am very grateful for that.

In August of last year, I began publishing a monthly newsletter, entitled, "Prison Epistle from ___ ____". I sent it to over 300 churches of Christ, mostly in North Carolina, but also in Tenn., Indiana, Oklahoma, and Ohio. I also began writing to many preachers in the brotherhood, but to my dismay, received almost no response. You can imagine my disappointment. I learned a valuable lesson. The church that exists today is not exactly like the first century A.D. church of Christ.

However, over the past three months, many men (_____) have appeared, as it seems, out of nowhere. I think that it has been a lesson in patience. I have been in prison going on seven years now; you would think that I would have learned how to be patient, huh? ...... Any way I actually received a tract that was personally sent by brother Hugo McCord. I am still at a loss how he received my address. ......"

This young brother continued on for another 4 pages, but one thought I feel must be passed on is the following:

"At the prison I just left, we had a very strong congregation. When I first began attending the church of Christ services there, there were only four or five men, and over a years' time, we had about ten faithful members of the Lord's people. I love them and miss them so very much! ......

When I arrived at this new prison camp in December, I was sad to leave my brethren behind, but was looking forward to the fellowship with a new congregation. Yet when I got here, I quickly realized that I was the only member of the Lord's church. ......"

The third letter that this young man wrote was one sent to Hugo McCord.[14]

"Dear Mr. McCord,

Greetings in the name of our Lord and master, Christ Jesus! My name is _____. I am 27 years old and I am currently serving a nine-year federal prison sentence for in _____ , _____ for drug distribution. I have been in prison for going on seven years now and have approximately eighteen months left until my release. I am writing to thank you so very much for the tract you sent me on preachers, I have read much of your work, and it was and is an honor to have received a package from you. I am not sure as to how you acquired my address. ...... I was going to write you last year, but because of the lack of response from so many other gospel preachers in the brotherhood, I decided not to write you. So please know how grateful I am that you contacted me. Words cannot express my gratitude.

......

I obeyed the gospel in 2001. Since then, I have been trying to prepare to

---

[14] I am grateful that brother McCord shared this letter with me.

preach upon my release. I really enjoy writing, so I spend a good deal of time writing on different scriptural topics. I hope to one day attain the writing skills that men like yourself, Guy N. Woods, J.W. McGarvey, etc., posses. I just want to do all that I can to effectively serve our Master with all of my heart and soul. I share the comments of the apostle Paul who said, '...... *woe is unto me, if I preach not the gospel!*' (I Cor. 9:16)

Over the past year, I have been writing to men in our brotherhood. Not asking for money or any material things. I simply need guidance. It is difficult to be in here all alone. I am so hungry, but I do not want to be led astray, something that I am on continual watch of.

......

I have been corresponding with James Meadows, David Pharr, Alan Highers and other preachers in North Carolina. All of these men have been very encouraging and helpful. I am very grateful for their time; something that I know they have very little of. I have submitted some of my papers to certain brotherhood publications hoping they possibly could be published. Brother Pharr is going to publish an article I wrote for the 'Carolina Messenger'. I have also written in the Carolina Christian. I

am very grateful for these men
thinking enough of what I have
written, to publish it. I really want to
contribute to the strengthening of the
kingdom. I read many brotherhood
publications. Since I have no
experience with the 'church of Christ'
outside of prison, I have been trying
to gain insight to what problems and
challenges I will be faced with as I am
released. It has been revealed to me,
that many in the brotherhood desire
to make the church that Christ
purchased with his blood (Acts 20:18)
a man-made denomination. This is
terribly disturbing to me. You see, all
I know is the Church is revealed in the
New Testament. It is one of such
glory, one that every sincere seeker of
God should strive to be a part.
However, many have their own
agenda, and this has historically been
the reason for so much division.

....

Upon my release, I am thinking
about going to East Tennessee School
of Preaching. I would like to attend
Freed Hardeman University and go to
graduate school as well. I have
obtained my Associates Degree since I
have been in prison.

I will call this brother, "Clifford" (as I have explained
earlier, I try not to use real names.) In his long letter, Clifford
makes it very clear that he asks for nothing but the "RIGHT HAND

OF FELLOWSHIP" of faithful children of God!

There is an old story about a sailing ship that was becalmed far from land and after many days, many birds took a small strand of string that as a whole, made up a rope, and pulled the ship to a place where the wind was blowing. Whereas just one bird could not budge the ship, the many could. Though this is just a 'fairy tale' the thought is a very true principle. There is reason for fellowship and that reason is to strengthen each other. As the gospel goes behind the iron bars and razor wire fences of prisons, it can and does touch the hearts of men and women. When these souls respond to the gospel they too need the encouragement of other Christians. But many times they do not receive this because they may be the only Christians in that facility.

The first problem that arises in starting any work in the Lord's vineyard is, finding the first individual that will give the teacher the time to present in a meaning and truthful presentation, the great story of the need of salvation, and the means by which that salvation is made possible. Though like the multitudes of this planet earth that go through life without ever giving any thought about God, Christ, their soul or eternity, there are men and women in our jails and prisons that continue with the same type of thinking.

It was for this reason (among others), that it was my good fortune to work with a congregation (the church in Owasso) who realized the importance of not just preaching and teaching first principals to inmates, but to show by their actions that Christians care not only for other Christians (which of course is true and needful), but also a care for the lost. This was one of the reasons that many members of the congregation, (and a few other congregations), engaged in what we called 'Adopt a prisoner picnic'. See some of these in the following photos:

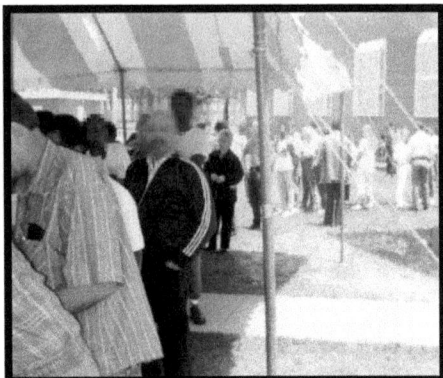

The congregation from Owasso, and members from other congregations (Broken Arrow, Atoka, Ada, Stratford, Oolagah, and one from the Oklahoma City area), had a part in such an activity. In two of the facilities we were allowed to do these for 10 years, and in two other facilities it was our joy to have such a meeting. At one of these facilities (a minimum facility) the warden granted us the privilege of inviting family members of the inmates to attend the gathering, and to stay for some two and half hours of gospel preaching, delivered by 5 different preachers from congregations located in Oklahoma City, Ada, Oolagah, and Tulsa.

I have received 3 letters in the past year that I believe will declare the importance and benefits of jail/prison evangelism. (Not just the efforts of the Owasso congregation, but the church as a whole.) Let's look at just a few of the thoughts of two inmates it was my joy to have had the opportunity to teach them about the Lord. Both were in the Tulsa County Jail, but separated by at least 10 or so years. One had served more than a dozen years in prison, while the other was in his first year of confinement.

This first letter comes from "Mitch", 'the newcomer' in the Oklahoma prison system. He writes:

> "I am still here at O.S.R. (Okla. State Reformatory) in Granit, and have met a friend of yours. His name is <u>Larry Brown</u> [of course not the real name] and he has written a letter accompany mine. (Inmates are very

careful with what little money they have, so one stamp to mail two letters is a great saving) I told him that I had met you J-6 (pod) of the Tulsa county jail in 2009. (This was several years after I had met Larry, my meeting with Larry was in the old Tulsa County Jail. *rdh*) ...... "Because of the Owasso's, and Bill Hamrick, I am working on my Bachelor's degree from Nations University. I am blessed to have had the opportunity to hear the word of God from you all! <u>Jim Pinkston</u> from Park Plaza too. .... Larry is a huge blessing to us here. He and I have often discussed the church of Christ, and the importance of the doctrines and truth that we both learned from your teaching." ...... Yours in Christ, <u>Mitch</u>.

In Mitch's second letter included the following thoughts;

"...... The volunteer here at O.S.R. is Larry Ware from the Granit church of Christ. He is very active here and I feel that God placed me here in part because of the influence <u>the church</u> of Christ has here. On the yard at Granite, the church meets every Sunday morning from 8:30 to 11:00 and are blessed to have the Lord's Supper and service every week!!! We also have 'New Life Behavior' classes twice a week, V.B.I. from

World Video Bible School classes as well. We are studying I Corinthians this session and are able to meet every Monday afternoon. What a blessing these videos are for us. ...... Thank you so much for all you do Ralph! With the guidance from you, Bill Hamrick, Jim Pinkston, Larry Ware, and the studies I am doing through Nations University, I am truly blessed.

Sincerely in Christ, Mitch

In the letter that Mitch mentioned from another inmate that it had been our pleasure and joy to teach, "Larry", these were some of the thoughts:

...... "Words cannot express how much you have blessed my life through the things I have experienced in the times we spent together talking about God's word. I am still growing because you planted that seed I needed to get the correct understanding of God's word that will have lasting power, and cannot be denied."

PRAYERS FOR PRISONERS – Owasso Church of Christ members wait to enter the Mack Alford Correction Center for the 2001 Adopt a Prisoner Picnic. They are, front from left, Diane Lynch, Jason Ketcherside, Kay Heinen, Marcia Ketcherside, Dakota Scribener, middle, Shirley Hunter, Matt Garner, Willene and Wayne Kroutil, Jack Martin, Tom Heinen, Robert Lawson, back, Paul Pickle, Richard Garner, David Whitt, Lyric Barnett, Dan Schnell, Sue Garner, Don Ketcherside, Tim Lunch and Vernon Bray. (submitted)

Church of Christ picnics at prisons

Owasso Church of Christ members recently attended the annual Adopt a Prisoner Picnic at the Mack Alford Correction Center in Stringtown.

The program enables members to worship with incarcerated Christians or other inmates involved in Bible study groups. Church members prepare lunch, have an hour of worship together and then have an hour of one-on-one visitation with prisoners.

"The rewards of this effort have included converts coming out of prison who are now preaching and teaching as faithful members of congregations in many places, and hope for men that will never walk free on the streets again," said Ralph Hunter, prison minister at the church. The congregation helped Hunter finance work at Mack Alford in 1984 and '85. In 1986 the church agreed to send Hunter into Oklahoma jails and prisons as a full-time missionary. Since then, he has ministered to inmates in Lexington, Joseph Harp, Jess Dunn, John Lillie, Mack Alford, McCleod, Rex Thompson, Tulsa County Jail and Avalon Center correctional facilities.